THE INTEGRATED LIFE OF
LEADERS

THE INTEGRATED LIFE OF LEADERS

Real Leaders.
Real Stories.
Real Impact.

ROGER OSBALDISTON

LEADER IMPACT PUBLISHING

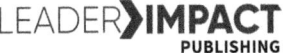

LEADER>IMPACT
PUBLISHING

The Integrated Life of Leaders: Real leaders. Real Stories. Real Impact.

Copyright © 2023 by LeaderImpact
All rights reserved. Neither this book, nor any parts within it may be sold or reproduced in any form or by any electronic or mechanical means, including information storage and retrieval systems, without permission in writing from the author. The only exception is by a reviewer, who may quote short excerpts in a review.

Scriptures taken from the Holy Bible, New International Version®, NIV®. Copyright © 1973, 1978, 1984, 2011 by Biblica, Inc.™ Used by permission of Zondervan. All rights reserved worldwide. www.zondervan.com The "NIV" and "New International Version" are trademarks registered in the United States Patent and Trademark Office by Biblica, Inc.™

Library of Congress Control Number: 2022952339

ISBN (hardcover): 9781662935060
ISBN (paperback): 9781662935077
eISBN: 9781662935084

This book is dedicated to leaders,

especially those who were willing to share their stories in this book.

It is a privilege to learn alongside you!

CONTENTS

	AUTHOR'S NOTE	9
	FOREWORD	10
	INTRODUCTION: THE PROBLEM WITH JUGGLING	12
1.	WIND IN YOUR SAILS	19
2.	KEEP CALM AND LEAD ON	31
3.	CHANGE OR DIE	43
4.	LET'S TALK	55
5.	SUCCESS	65
6.	MONEY, MONEY, MONEY	75
7.	RISKY BUSINESS	85
8.	HONEY, I'M HOME!	95
9.	BETTER TOGETHER	105
10.	POSITIVE IMPACT	117
	ABOUT LEADERIMPACT	129
	ACKNOWLEDGMENTS	131
	ABOUT THE AUTHOR	133
	ENDNOTES	134
	WOULD YOU LIKE TO KNOW GOD PERSONALLY?	139
	HAVE YOU MADE THE WONDERFUL DISCOVERY OF THE SPIRIT-FILLED LIFE?	159

AUTHOR'S NOTE

It is my great privilege to share with you in this book the real stories of real leaders making a real impact around the world.

This book has been designed to be read one chapter at a time, with a chance to reflect on it and hopefully discuss with others.

My "recommended dose" is that you take one chapter per week, along with a few other people, and discuss it as you go.

That should prevent the cognitive indigestion that can sometimes come from reading books too quickly!

Enjoy!

Roger

FOREWORD

In his book, *The Integrated Life of Leaders*, Roger Osbaldiston provides great insights on how to lead a life that is whole, wholesome, and effective. The style of this book makes it easy to read. At the same time, the richness of the concepts he unlocks calls for deep reflections and applications. This book provides a simple, but adequate philosophical framework for integrating our personal, professional, and spiritual lives.

In a complex and dynamic world, there are no simple paths to ensuring success in both our personal and professional lives. Osbaldiston illustrates the way to an integrated life and leadership through the stories of professionals from different regions of the world. The stories are about real people, real struggles, and real victories. The vulnerability with which these leaders share their struggles is motivated by the common desire to be of help to others. But more importantly, they are inviting interested readers who want to positively impact their spheres of influence to join the LeaderImpact network.

By joining this global network, you will find the relational support and other resources that can propel your life and leadership to greater heights of significance and effectiveness. What is even more exciting is that from your relationships with your organization, with your city, and with your nation, you will be among men and women who are impacting and changing our world for good. I encourage you to digest the gems in this book and join the global network of integrated leaders who are on the faith adventure of impacting their world with Jesus Christ.

Prof. Delanyo Adadevoch
President of the International Leadership Foundation

INTRODUCTION: THE PROBLEM WITH JUGGLING

Not my circus, not my monkeys.

—*Polish proverb*

HOW GOOD ARE YOU AT JUGGLING?

Unless you have a past career as a circus clown, I would guess that your juggling skills might be a bit like mine. I can manage a couple of balls at a time, but when the number increases significantly, I am more than likely to end up on the floor with balls raining down on me.

The same may be true in life and leadership. As leaders, we seem to face an ever-increasing set of demands, challenges, opportunities, and problems. This is not just in our professional world—it's all of life: work, family, staying healthy, finances, and endless opportunities to serve in our communities.

How can we manage it all? How do we make a difference? How can we create a positive impact without becoming overwhelmed?

This book seeks to unpack the nature of the challenges we face, explore the foundation of what I believe is the secret to an integrated and impactful life, and introduce you to a community of other leaders who are intentional about living in an integrated way, in various contexts and aspects of life and leadership. Throughout the book we will meet business people, doctors, and charity sector leaders seeking to create positive impact while leading integrated, fulfilling lives.

WE CAN'T DO IT ALL

I have a confession.

I am not Superman. To be honest, most days I'm not sure I can even match Clark Kent. Yet, at the same time, I feel like I ought to be saving the world.

I suspect a lot of us leaders have a desire to have an impact on the world, to make a difference, and leave a lasting legacy—but we can feel overwhelmed by the regular challenges of everyday life. Sometimes these challenges seem to prevent us from realizing our full potential.

Is it actually possible to make a positive impact with our lives while also trying to just make life work?

I believe it is. But I also believe that we can't do it all. And we were never meant to.

Trying to "do it all" is not only exhausting, as we are pulled apart in competing directions, but it is also ultimately ineffective as we seek to do a little of everything.

BURNT OUT IN BARCELONA

Barcelona is one of my favorite cities. I love the Gaudí architecture, the narrow lanes of the Barri Gotic, the gastronomy of the many restaurant options, and the beaches that spread for miles along the warm Mediterranean coast. However, on one visit, instead of enjoying the Hotel Mediterraneo where I was staying, I was experiencing an attack of anxiety, and I could not sleep without my mind filling with dread and panic.

I had flown from my home in New Zealand to Barcelona to participate in a weeklong global task force meeting. It was the second time that year.

I was exhausted from traveling. Did I mention yet that Barcelona is on the exact opposite side of the world to my home in New Zealand, a mere twenty thousand kilometers away? I had just finished leading a day of meetings, and as evening approached, I felt a wave of anxiety and panic come over me. I thought I was probably dying of a heart attack: tight chest, light-headedness, sweating. I contacted a doctor, and after a while he assured me that my heart was just fine and that I was most likely experiencing an anxiety attack.

I had never experienced anything like this before. My life until then had almost always been on the go, moving forward, moving up, leading, achieving . . . I thought I was pretty much invincible. I was wrong.

I was thirty-four years old, leading a team of about sixty staff, and we had been experiencing incredible growth and expansion. This had meant lots of travel, and my body had decided it was time to remind me that I was human and that enough was enough. I also had a young family at home—my wonderful wife and two young sons—and always a few home projects on the go. Yet here I was, on the other side of the world, and I thought that my life was over!

Well, my life was not over. In fact, my experience in Barcelona began a much deeper journey into understanding myself and reflecting on how to live a life of active leadership in a more integrated and fruitful way. It also drove me deeper into my relationship with God and dependence on him and his Spirit. This journey has taught me the secret of living a more integrated and impactful life, and I look forward to sharing more of this in the coming chapters as we meet other leaders who have also learned similar lessons.

MAXIMUM IMPACT

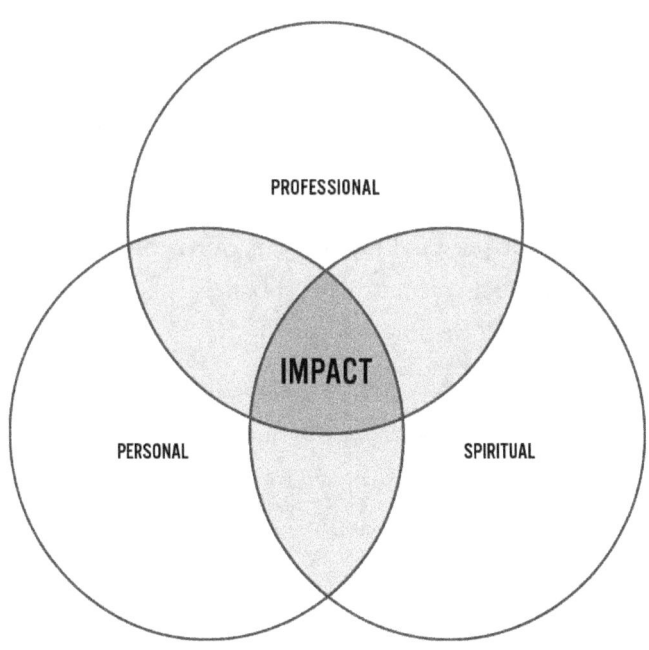

I had the immense privilege of being the global executive director for LeaderImpact from 2019 to 2023. LeaderImpact is a multinational network of leaders who seek to have a positive impact on the world around them. In his book, *Becoming a Leader of Impact*,[1] Braden Douglas outlines the foundational philosophy of LeaderImpact. The essence of this philosophy is that in order to have our maximum impact as leaders, our lives need to be integrated. This involves bringing all aspects of our lives together, whether they be personal, professional, or spiritual.

No diagram can ever completely describe the many facets and complexity of our human experience, but this simple diagram has been very helpful to me. This diagram says three things to me:

1. We are complex people! Every aspect of our lives is interconnected and integrated. We may each use different categories to describe the various aspects of lives; however, these three categories cover a lot of bases for me.

2. We cannot separate out parts of our lives and view them as separate. We cannot succeed in one part of life and fail in another and keep them from impacting each other—for long. Our personal life impacts our professional life, and our spiritual convictions and beliefs (or absence of them) influence all we do.

3. The intersection space of a diagram like this describes the outcome of the integration and intersection of them all. As leaders, our best impact and influence will occur when we bring together the best of all our selves—our integrated selves.

THE PROBLEM WITH BALANCE

One thing I want to avoid implying here is that life needs to be "balanced." Balance can tend to imply that there are several equally important aspects to life that we must seek to keep in balance all the time. An integrated life is not about keeping everything in balance.

Often, one aspect of our lives may need more attention than another. This can change throughout our lives and in the different seasons of life, such as parenting and times of crisis or health challenges. The important thing is to know what needs attention at a given time. For example, if you are in a start-up business, it will take more emotional energy than it might once you get more established. If your teenage children are struggling at the same time, you have a leader-sized challenge to stay integrated. Sometimes this means life will feel very out of balance, even when we are focusing on the right things.

WHAT IS INTEGRATION?

As we talk more about an integrated life, it's worth asking the question, "What does *integration* mean?"

Our word *integrated* comes originally from the Latin word *integer*, meaning "untouched, entire, complete." It is also central to mathematics.

Another derived meaning comes from psychology: "the organization of the constituent elements of the personality into a coordinated, harmonious whole."[2] The opposite of this would be *disintegration*, where we feel like we are tearing ourselves apart and destroying ourselves.

That is what we are hoping to avoid, yet it is also where many of us tend to find ourselves at times.

To live an integrated life means to live in a harmonious and sustainable way that brings together all elements of our lives. It also results in us living and leading in a way that feels complete and whole, as opposed to feeling like we are being torn apart in different directions.

It is almost as if we could live as we were designed and created to—but that's a topic for the next chapter! Perhaps there is a secret to being integrated and being able to do all we are intended to do, without the need to juggle like a circus clown.

1.
WIND IN YOUR SAILS

When you can't change the direction of the wind, adjust your sails.

—H. Jackson Brown Jr.[3]

BECALMED

Living in the South Pacific gives us close access to several beautiful Pacific Islands. On one trip to Fiji with my wife, Nicki, we decided to try our hand at sailing.

Incidentally, I love the song by Crosby Stills and Nash called "Southern Cross,"[4] which paints a simple, lyrical picture of a sleek yacht riding the ocean breeze . . .

Eighty feet of the waterline, nicely making way.

Back in Fiji, we chose one of our resort's free Hobie Cats and pushed offshore—and okay, it probably had less than eighteen feet of waterline, let alone eighty. Still, we caught a nice little offshore breeze that took us out near the edge of the lagoon, sailing away, me showing my wife my instantly acquired sailing skills . . . until we stopped. Dead still.

The nice little breeze had gone, and we found ourselves becalmed. Now, the lagoon was very shallow, and we could probably have just swum or walked back, but I thought it best to at least bring the Hobie Cat back to the resort. So we waited . . . and waited. Finally, a little *off*shore breeze came back . . . but we wanted to go *on*shore, not *off*. Eventually, we worked it out and managed to point the boat into the breeze and get back to the beach. We haven't tried that again. And we are still married.

My home country, New Zealand, is well known for having some of the best sailors in the world; however, as you have picked up by now, I am not one of them. But the fact remains that even the best sailor in the world cannot go far if there is no wind. The power of the wind is a critical factor.

I think the same is true for our life, leadership, and living an integrated life.

As leaders, we need real wind in our sails—a power that goes beyond what we can humanly possess. This is where the spiritual side of life is vital. A truly integrated life is also a Spirit-filled life. I personally believe it is no surprise that in the Bible, the Greek word used for *Spirit* (and the *Holy Spirit*) is *pneuma*, which means "wind, or breath." The presence of God, in the form of the Holy Spirit in our life, can sometimes seem vague or ethereal. However, as we understand more about God through reading his Word, the Bible, and by talking with others who follow him, his presence becomes more and more tangible.

As people and leaders, just as we were never meant to live without the physical breath of life, neither are we meant to live without the spiritual side of life. We are dependent on the "filling" of our lives with the Spirit of God. Just as much as God created us to breathe physically, we need to breathe spiritually—to be filled with his Spirit, a "wind" that can give real power to our sails. By allowing ourselves to be filled with the Holy Spirit, we experience God's power in our lives and are able to realize a greater impact that we could on our own.

When we open up to the spiritual side of life, then we can become fully integrated and able to live the life of leadership that God has always intended. I believe only God's Spirit can give us the power to live as truly integrated and authentic leaders.

Of course, not everyone who is reading this book is a follower of Jesus Christ like me or has considered pursuing the spiritual side of life, but if you will allow me, I would like the chance to encourage you to consider the importance of the spiritual. In particular, I would like to encourage you to consider the life of Jesus as a model for an integrated life. Both I and the other leaders we will meet in this book may use examples of Jesus's life and leadership as we illustrate the integrated life of leaders.

At this point you may be asking, "What is the Spirit-filled life Roger is talking about?"

Great question!

LeaderImpact has a series of resources that can help us understand the spiritual side of life, and one of these is called "Five Truths."[5] In this guide, there is a good summary of the Spirit-filled life:

When you decide to follow Jesus, the Holy Spirit comes to live inside you. This means you can be in constant relationship with the Father. Not only that, but the Spirit gives us power to live lives of true significance that makes a difference in our lives, our relationships, and the world around us. While every believer is indwelt by the Holy Spirit, being empowered by the Holy Spirit is a choice that we make on a daily basis. The Bible calls this empowerment "filling," so being "Spirit-filled" means to be controlled and empowered by the Holy Spirit.*

CARRIED ALONG

The Bible also contains a sailing story that ended a little more dramatically than my Fijian sailing experience. We can find it in the Bible in the book of Acts, chapter 27, where the missionary Paul sets sail from Israel for Rome. Take a moment to enjoy this story:

> When it was decided that we would sail for Italy, Paul and some other prisoners were handed over to a centurion named Julius, who belonged to the Imperial Regiment. We boarded a ship from Adramyttium about to sail for ports along the coast of the province of Asia, and we put out to sea.

---

* If you would like a more detailed explanation of how to begin a relationship with God like this and how to be filled with the Holy Spirit, you may like to check out the appendices in this book titled "Would You Like to Know God Personally?" and "Have You Made the Wonderful Discovery of the Spirit-Filled Life?" Used with permission from CruPress.

The next day we landed at Sidon. From there we put out to sea again and passed to the lee of Cyprus because the winds were against us. When we had sailed across the open sea off the coast of Cilicia and Pamphylia, we landed at Myra in Lycia. There the centurion found an Alexandrian ship sailing for Italy and put us on board. We made slow headway for many days and had difficulty arriving off Cnidus. When the wind did not allow us to hold our course, we sailed to the lee of Crete, opposite Salmone. We moved along the coast with difficulty and came to a place called Fair Havens, near the town of Lasea.

Much time had been lost, and sailing had already become dangerous. Paul warned them, "Men, I can see that our voyage is going to be disastrous and bring great loss to ship and cargo, and to our own lives also." But the centurion, instead of listening to what Paul said, followed the advice of the pilot and of the owner of the ship. Since the harbor was unsuitable to winter in, the majority decided that we should sail on, hoping to reach Phoenix and winter there. This was a harbor in Crete, facing both southwest and northwest.

When a gentle south wind began to blow, they saw their opportunity; so, they weighed anchor and sailed along the shore of Crete. Before very long, a wind of hurricane force, called the Northeaster, swept down from the island. The ship was caught by the storm and could not head into the wind; so, we gave way to it and were *driven along*. As we passed to the lee of a small island called Cauda, we were hardly able to make the lifeboat secure, so the men hoisted it aboard. Then they passed ropes under the ship itself to hold it together. Because they were afraid they would run aground on the sandbars of Syrtis, they lowered the sea anchor and let the ship be *driven along*. We took such a violent battering from the storm that the next day they began to throw the cargo overboard. On the third day, they threw the ship's tackle overboard with their own hands. When neither sun nor stars appeared for many days and the storm continued raging, we finally gave up all hope of being saved.

After they had gone a long time without food, Paul stood up before them and said: "Men, you should have taken my advice not to sail from Crete; then you would have spared yourselves this damage and loss. But now I urge you to keep up your courage, because not one of you will be lost; only the ship will be destroyed. Last night an angel of the God to whom I belong and whom I serve stood beside me and said, 'Do not be afraid, Paul. You must stand trial before Caesar; and God has graciously given you the lives of all who sail with you.' So keep up your courage, men, for I have faith in God that it will happen just as he told me. Nevertheless, we must run aground on some island."

On the fourteenth night we were still being driven across the Adriatic Sea, when about midnight the sailors sensed they were approaching land. They took soundings and found that the water was a hundred and twenty feet deep. A short time later they took soundings again and found it was ninety feet deep. Fearing that we would be dashed against the rocks, they dropped four anchors from the stern and prayed for daylight. In an attempt to escape from the ship, the sailors let the lifeboat down into the sea, pretending they were going to lower some anchors from the bow. Then Paul said to the centurion and the soldiers, "Unless these men stay with the ship, you cannot be saved." So the soldiers cut the ropes that held the lifeboat and let it drift away.

Just before dawn Paul urged them all to eat. "For the last fourteen days," he said, "you have been in constant suspense and have gone without food—you haven't eaten anything. Now I urge you to take some food. You need it to survive. Not one of you will lose a single hair from his head." After he said this, he took some bread and gave thanks to God in front of them all. Then he broke it and began to eat. They were all encouraged and ate some food themselves. Altogether there were 276 of us on board. When they had eaten as much as they wanted, they lightened the ship by throwing the grain into the sea.

When daylight came, they did not recognize the land, but they saw a bay with a sandy beach, where they decided to run the ship aground if they could. Cutting loose the anchors, they left them in the sea and at the same time untied the ropes that held the rudders. Then they hoisted the foresail to the wind and made for the beach. But the ship struck a sandbar and ran aground. The bow stuck fast and would not move, and the stern was broken to pieces by the pounding of the surf.

The soldiers planned to kill the prisoners to prevent any of them from swimming away and escaping. But the centurion wanted to spare Paul's life and kept them from carrying out their plan. He ordered those who could swim to jump overboard first and get to land. The rest were to get there on planks or on other pieces of the ship. In this way everyone reached land safely.[6] (Emphasis mine.)

What a dramatic sailing story! A storm, a shipwreck in an unknown island, and yet all 276 people on board landed safely. Remarkable.

What stood out to you from the story?

There are lots of great insights we can gain from this story. However, there is one image, a simple phrase, that I want to draw out from this story. In facing the storm, it says they decided to let the boat give way, or surrendered to the wind, and let the boat be "driven along." Rather than try and fight the wind, the sailors gave up, surrendered to the power of the wind, and let the boat be carried along by the wind.

Just as the wind can carry along a boat, so too the power of God can empower and carry us along—if we are prepared to "let go" and surrender to the power of God in our lives. It is worth noting that, while the sailors in this story were desperate, and we certainly have desperate times on occasion, the need to surrender to God's power is constant. A habit of turning to God in surrender is needful in all situations.

This chapter in Acts was originally written in the Greek language, and it is the word *phero* that is translated in English as being "driven along."

This same Greek word is also found in another part of the Bible to describe how people were *"carried along* by the Holy Spirit"[7] (emphasis mine) as they wrote the words of the Bible.

As leaders, we have the same opportunity to be "carried along," empowered by the Spirit of God.

Too many times, we simply attempt to power our own boat. It's like we sometimes choose to ignore the powerful wind, put out our small oars, and proceed to paddle against the wind, rather than harness the immense power of the wind to propel us forward with much greater speed.

This is a consistent theme in the Bible, and it comes out again in the letter of Ephesians chapter 5 where the writer encourages the recipients to be "filled with the Spirit"—the same sense of being under the power, influence, and direction of the Spirit. He talks elsewhere about the "fruit of the spirit" that can come from being "filled with the Spirit": love, joy, peace, patience, kindness, goodness, faithfulness, gentleness, and self-control.

If you ever wanted to be a leader who demonstrates and possesses more love, joy, peace, patience, kindness, goodness, faithfulness, gentleness, or self-control, the secret is not more self-effort, self-help books or courses, or therapy. I believe the answer is to be filled with the Spirit of God, who can help us produce this kind of spiritual fruit.

Jesus said this himself in the Gospel of John 15:5:

> I am the vine; you are the branches. If you remain in me and I in you, you will bear much fruit.

For a branch, fruit comes naturally from staying connected to the sustenance of vine, in this case Jesus. The branch does not need to work hard to produce good fruit if it just stays connected to the source. In the same way, we produce fruit as we are filled with the Spirit of Jesus.

WORK SMARTER, NOT HARDER

As I mentioned in the chapter before, I worked really hard in the early years of my leadership to be successful, which did lead to success, but it also led to burnout! Over the years since, I have learned more and more how to let go and be "carried along" by the Spirit, to listen to what God wants for my life, focus on those things, and trust him for even greater fruitfulness.

I think this is a great example of what it could be like to work much, much smarter, not just harder.

In summary of this section, a truly integrated life for a leader must also include the spiritual side of life. Growing personally and professionally as leaders is not enough on its own if we truly want to lead an integrated life of greatest impact. It is only as we discover and live a Spirit-filled life that we can be fully integrated and fruitful as we face the challenges and issues of life and our tasks as leaders.

Over the coming chapters, we will explore the real stories of real leaders who are making a real impact around the world. These stories have been shared with openness and vulnerability, because these leaders believe what I believe: that growing personally, professionally, and spiritually and helping others to do the same is a worthwhile endeavor. Together, we will explore several topics that every leader will regularly face, and we will approach them, not just to discover insights in dealing with each issue, but to also consider how we can approach them as leaders seeking to live a truly integrated life.

* * *

Questions for Discussion:

1. Where do you look to find the motivation and energy for your life and leadership?
2. Are you experiencing "wind in your sails" from the spiritual side of your life? If so, how have you seen this in your life?
3. What is one step you can take to move closer to growing more spiritually?

2.
KEEP CALM AND LEAD ON

Everybody has plans until they get hit for the first time.

—*Mike Tyson*[8]

STRESSED OUT

I feel like I have battled stress most of my life. As I mentioned in the introduction, at one point it pushed me into a period of burnout, kick-started by a trip to Barcelona.

I have also had periods of significant stress over the years that stemmed from leadership roles I have been in. I haven't always handled it well, and I still battle anxiety and its effects, which come from an accumulation of stressors.

Some stress and the related anxiety, burnout, and even depression can come from deciding to keep doing things we really don't want to do, have the energy for, or are not gifted for.

The Irish poet David Whyte recalls returning home one day after another tiring day of working and then having the chance to spend time with his friend Brother D. Steindl Rast.[9]

David said to him, "Speak to me about exhaustion."

Brother Rast, a Benedictine monk, told him, "The antidote to exhaustion is not necessarily rest, it's wholeheartedness. The reason you are so exhausted is that much of what you are doing, you have no affection for."

Loving what you do—having an affection for it and a confidence that you are in the right place and doing the right things—is critical when your work and leadership inevitably produce stress.

One of the leaders I admire in this respect is Braden Douglas. I first met Braden in 2006 on a visit to Canada, and since then, we have found ourselves collaborating on a number of projects. I remember him saying to me once, "If something doesn't blow your hair back, don't do it!" Judging by the state of my hair, I must have done a lot of these things!

Braden always strikes me as a very positive, energetic, and confident leader. Yet he also shared with me about how he deals with stress in his life and business—especially when things don't always go the way we hope.

In 2018, everything really seemed to be going according to plan for Braden and his firm.

Sure, the business had its ups and downs, and the young marketing company never seemed to have a surplus of time or money, but they were growing and managing that tension. Then 2018 hit, and they lost a few clients. The losses weren't due to any catastrophic event, the economy, or even a market shift. There were several different scenarios: one company got bought out and changed their marketing firm; another company decided to open their own marketing department. It was just that they came at the same time and together caused major stress for Braden, the founder and CEO.

Braden had started Crew Marketing Partners in 2007. It was an inauspicious beginning. In fact, it started in Braden's basement. He hired his first employee a month later and hired an average of one employee per quarter for the next several years. So in 2018, Braden was responsible for offices in three cities and fifty employees. With the client losses, they were running out of money and the payroll was every two weeks. Crew needed at least $150,000 to $170,000 in the bank just to make payroll.

This began a downward spiral where, short on cash, the company took on a line of credit. Braden was trying to get new clients, but that was not an instant process, and they simply didn't come quickly enough. The tension built, and then came the day when he realized they would have to start laying people off. This naturally made everyone in the company take notice, and then others started to leave when they thought their position might not be as secure as they had hoped. This then meant they were shorthanded and struggling to get any of their work done.

Braden put his savings into the company and then had to have the difficult discussion with Jen, his wife, about taking out a second mortgage on their home. The bank refused more credit, they were just about out of cash completely, and then the doubts started.

Braden recalls thinking, *What is going on? Maybe I'm just not a good entrepreneur. I can't believe I allowed us to get into this!*

His employees were getting mad. He had suppliers who were getting mad at not being paid on time; the pressure cooker of stress was tense at home as well as at work.

Braden tells us, "That's when I started to ask, 'Okay, where is God in this?'"

When Braden was in high school, he was not a person of faith, but he recalls praying at exam time. He said many of his friends tried to bargain with God for answers on a math exam, but it didn't work. He knew if it didn't work that way back in high school, it still might not work that way now.

If we are honest with ourselves, we must admit that sometimes we want the quick fix. In most cases, stress is an invitation to Holy Spirit–dependent leadership. Braden realized he had no choice but to lead through it. The difference in Braden's case is, he realized that in order to lead through it, he needed to draw off his spiritual orientation and the filling of the Holy Spirit. As a result, he learned several principles along the way about dealing with stress as a leader.

LOVE WHAT YOU DO

Braden loves business. He loves entrepreneurs and marketplace leaders because, in his words, "They have a greater opportunity to impact the world than they think they know. And if we can help them make money as a company and use their platform for good, that's how they can make a significant impact."

Because Braden loves what he does, and because he feels called to it, he was willing to do the hard stuff, managing the stress and coming out to the other end.

Having the confidence that you are doing what you love and are supposed to be doing is foundational to having the strength that leadership requires. Spending the time working through a personal mission statement and clarifying your purpose in life will help strengthen you for the stress ahead.

STRESS REVEALS CHARACTER

There is a principle in Christianity that says anything that we value more than God and our relationship with him is an idol. The Bible has a lot to say about worshipping idols rather than God. In Braden Douglas's case, the stress of that period of seven or eight months in 2018 revealed that he had placed his business and success as an idol in his life.

Braden recalls thinking, "If my business was successful, I was successful and I was worthy and was worth something. But what if it was taken away? And what if I were financially ruined? What I realized was that my character and identity were wrapped up in the success of my business and being able to tell people, 'Oh yeah, we're a great company, and we're growing and doing all these great things.' And I realized that my identity was rooted in the business and my success as a leader, where it should have been in my relationship with God and who he says I am."

Dealing with stress as a leader is part of the process used to define who we are. It *reveals* our character and where our identity as a person is rooted. It also *shapes* our identity and character. Braden learned from those lessons and is a better leader today because of it. Being willing to face ourselves and the character revealed by stress may be uncomfortable, but it also makes the stress worth the effort.

A good way to evaluate our character during stressful situations is to step back and consider what our internal and external responses reveal about us. That is not to say that a bit of worry isn't normal or healthy. Stress can be good or bad. Feeling pressured to make payroll should be a good motivator to focus on growing the business and not overspending. Being so tied up with worry that we are unable to take action reveals something else, and we need to find out what that is.

There is also an interesting balance to our external responses. It is good to be honest and to acknowledge our fears or stresses within the context of safe relationships. On the other hand, it is equally important to be a confident leader, even in the face of obvious challenges, in order to give others the security to move forward. If your employees know that you know what the financial situation is and that you are concerned about it, but that you also remain calm and reassuring, they will want to contribute and go the extra mile themselves.

One more thought on character: What you project to others should be real. In other words, if your demeanor, words, and actions are just a false front that you are projecting, people will sense it. Conversely, if you are being real and authentic, revealing your honest concerns and also projecting hope, people will be much more likely to relax and perform well.

STRENGTH IN A SAFE COMMUNITY

Braden was involved in a LeaderImpact small group during that tense time in 2018. During that time, when he needed to project a calm confidence to his employees and clients, it was very helpful to have a group of fellow entrepreneurs to meet with weekly. During those group times, he could share some of his fears or anxiety. It was important to have a place where he could work things out mentally without fear of judgment.

Through his LeaderImpact group, Braden experienced the concept of community on an entirely different level. While he was working out payroll and bank loans, he had a group of peers reminding him of where his true identity was rooted. They would ask questions like, "Hey, what's God really teaching you through this?" or even, "Why are you still struggling with this?"

Braden remembers that time and reflects, "There's a common accountability, a group where you can actually bring in the spiritual life in a very authentic way, that makes it much richer."

STRESS IS INTEGRATED

One of the basic truths of life is that as much as we think we can compartmentalize and keep our personal and professional lives separate, we are still only one person. Who we are at home affects who we are at work and vice versa. When you bring the spiritual into the mix, you have all the key factors, and the big question is how well you integrate those distinct parts.

In Braden's case, his stress at work affected his relationships and even his finances in his personal life. Conversely, how his wife, Jen, responded to the financial stress affected how Braden approached things at work. Because the stress affected all of Braden's life—personally, professionally, and spiritually—the solutions and working out of that stress were integrated as well.

Braden realized this at the time and reflects, "We are not individual compartments that move from work to home life to church life. I find that when you start to really peel back professional, personal, and your spiritual life and who you are and what you believe, that starts to tell a bigger and better story."

This leads us to an approach that really helps when going through stressful times. If our stress is work-related, for example, asking ourselves how it may be affecting those we love or our own mental health is a great start in integrating. When we ask ourselves how the stress is affecting how we feel about ourselves and what we believe, we can begin to get a healthier perspective and the objectivity that will see us through the challenges.

SPIRITUAL BREATHING HELPS

We don't even think about breathing. It is a natural thing that we do instinctively. There is also a concept called "spiritual breathing," which takes a little more thought and intentionality.[10] The idea is that when physically breathing, we exhale the bad air and inhale the good air, giving our body what we need to survive. Spiritually speaking, we exhale, or confess, the attitudes or actions that are not pleasing to God and certainly not helping us deal with life in an effective manner. When we inhale spiritually, we take in the things that are true. Here is an example of how someone might do this in prayer.

> **Exhale**: "Lord, I am worried that we are not going to make it financially. I'm concerned that I'm not a good enough leader to see our team through this situation. What if I fail and have to close my company? I'll never be able to live it down!"

Inhale: "But, Lord, you know what is going on here better than I do. You are not surprised by the downturn in the economy, and it is no accident that you have me in this position to give leadership. The most important thing here is to do my best and trust you. Thank you that you love me and my worth is not based on what others think of me, or even how I feel about myself. Help me to see you at work here and to be sensitive to others in the process."

Braden Douglas's experience helps us to understand that while stress can be either positive or negative, it can always be instructive. We learn a lot about ourselves through stress. Sometimes we handle it well, and other times not so much. Being a leader of impact means we keep on trying, working through the hard stuff, and learning all we can.

In Braden's case, the stress of 2018 wasn't fatal to Crew Marketing Partners. Within a few months, the business stabilized, and they have continued to expand.

Things don't always work out so well. Sometimes, regardless of how good a leader we are, we fail. There are no guarantees. The real victory comes in using the stress to grow and continue to add value to the world around us. The biggest long-term impact of the events of 2018 was what happened in Braden's life as a result of this time. While stress revealed Braden's character at the time, it also provided a growth opportunity, and that is always part of becoming a leader of impact.

Stress reveals character and beliefs—what we really believe about ourselves.

THE TRUTH WILL SET YOU FREE

Psychologists also tell me there can be three levels to dealing with some stress:

- Behavior level—changing what we do
- Thoughts-and-feelings level—changing what we think and feel
- Beliefs level—changing what we believe

For me, some of the most stressful parts of leadership have been around conflict and interpersonal relationships. I remember, during one of these stress-filled periods, I had tried to alter my *behavior* and manage my time and commitments better. Yet doing this alone did nothing to change me in the long term, so I began to get help to process my *thoughts and feelings*.

This was helpful to a point, but I didn't make real progress until a counselor helped me to see that my behavior, thoughts, and feelings come from my *beliefs*.

I needed to discover *why* I felt motivated to do the things I did, and this came from beliefs hidden below the surface in the subconscious. I had to get to the level of my deepest motivations.

So I began to trace my behaviors, thoughts, and feelings back to the things I subconsciously believed about God, myself, and the world and to replace my false and unhelpful beliefs with truth.

This made all the difference in the world!

As leaders, we need to trade our self-made beliefs and self-talk for what is actually true about us and the world. As Jesus said,

You will know the truth, and the truth will set you free.[11]

In Braden Douglas's case, he was willing to face the truth about the stress he was facing with his company and how it was affecting his family. He integrated his spiritual life in the mix and discovered how he had let his position become an idol and determine his own sense of self. As he began to be honest with himself, he began to lead with more humility and confidence. He realized that what he believed about his worth in God's eyes was going to either propel him forward or hold him back.

The result was positive, not only in his personal life, but also as he saw the company turn around. Again, there were several factors in this turnaround, and there were no guarantees of success. The main thing was, his willingness to address reality made it possible for him to do his best and be at peace with the outcome.

* * *

Questions for Discussion:

1. What role does stress play in your life? Do you feel like you handle stress well, or can it be overwhelming and impact your whole life?

2. Think of a time when leading was stressful for you. What helped you get through that time? Did you ever sense that God was present with you during this time?

3. Which insight from Braden about dealing with stress is the most helpful for you?

4. Do you love what you do? Can you explain why?

3.
CHANGE OR DIE

The best way to predict the future is to invent it.

—*Alan Kay*[12]

My friend Don Van Meer was the CEO of a company called Carswell, a division of Thomson Reuters. Carswell had been in Canada since 1864 providing resources, services, and support primarily to legal practitioners and organizations across Canada in a range of formats—including books, loose-leaf services, journals, and newsletters.

For the first 130 years of their business, the way people consumed information was exactly the same: the printed page. And then, as the sheer volume of information they needed to access began to dramatically increase, customers had a need for information solutions that integrated content and technology. Nimble start-ups were attempting to respond, and they started to see a major change in the industry—competitors who had not previously existed were suddenly threatening their leading market share position.

Don had previously been the vice president of finance but had been appointed as president and CEO when all this change became obvious. Don and his leadership team realized that there was going to be a day when the traditional publishing model would be obsolete.

The impact of this technological shift was going to be fundamental to their business. They were faced with the choice of competing against their leading position in the traditional space or watching a competitor take the market share from them. They realized that to make this transition, they were going to have to fundamentally change every process in their business. They were going to have to change the roles of half their staff—meaning five hundred plus people—overnight. They were going to have to develop new competencies in technology and completely change their fee structures. They were facing at least two or three years of transition, taking a highly profitable business (which they believed was doomed without significant change) and turning it into something new.

Don says, "We were going to have to build a technological competency that didn't even exist. We were going to have to challenge a highly profitable business with high margins and start producing high-cost products, which in the short term would not cover the investment required. The impact would be that customers were going to cancel the high-profit-margin print products that Carswell was delivering and, instead, purchase these low-margin, high-cost products that we were now needing to develop. If Carswell was successful in the short term, revenue was going to remain flat, and there would be a significant drop in our margins.

If we didn't make the change though, Carswell would ultimately lose the market share and would likely never recover."

Essentially for Carswell, it was either change or die.

ENERGIZED OR PARALYZED

In describing this process, Don quotes Jack Welch, who said, "Anytime there is change, there is an opportunity. So it is paramount that an organization get energized rather than paralyzed."[13]

Don and Carswell got energized. Not only did they transition to a new business model, the broader company, Thomson Reuters, continues to be the world's leading source of intelligent information for businesses and professionals.

Yet probably the most astounding thing to me about their process is that through the change, Carswell was also named as one of Canada's 50 Best Employers by *The Globe and Mail Report on Business Magazine* in 2004, 2005, and 2006. *Maclean's* magazine also named Carswell one of Canada's Top 100 Employers for six consecutive years.

How did they transform their business and work so radically and successfully and at the same time keep their people energized, engaged, and on their side?

Don would be the first to recognize the commitment and engagement of his entire leadership team. Carswell's success can also be attributed to Don, as an individual leader, understanding and living an integrated life. In addition to understanding the professional and technical changes that the business would need to make, there were personal and spiritual aspects to Don's life that impacted his leadership. He understood that the changes needed to take place in his company were not just based on technical knowledge or skill. It would take something more.

GET IT, FEEL IT, WANT IT

The process Don led the team through at Carswell involved three dimensions of change. The first is *cognitive understanding*, defined as "knowing what the organization's strategic goals and values are." The second dimension is having an *emotional attachment*. This happens when your staff actually care about the business they're in and want to be a part of it. The third dimension is that they have *motivation*. They have the drive to want to succeed and want to be part of the solution as opposed to being part of the problem. Simply put, Don wanted his staff to "*get it, feel it, and want it.*"

A big part of people "getting it" is helping your team understand the context of the change. People often feel like, "Why are you doing this to me? I loved my job yesterday. Today you just come in and announce that you are making all these massive changes . . . I don't even know what I'm supposed to do."

So at Carswell, Don started talking about the changes that were happening in the marketplace and what their customers were saying they needed. All their people did not necessarily agree with the company leadership, but at least they understood why they were making the changes they were making.

In Don's words, "One of the things I learned was that employees honestly don't expect perfection from leadership. We're humans. We are not going to be right all the time. But they do expect honesty. Our employees want to look at us as leaders and say, 'I believe in the integrity of this person.'"

Change is just not about leaders taking people through something. Change is about engaging people in the process of change; having them be part of the decision-making; having them understand where you are going as an organization; having them buy into the process, even when they don't understand all of it.

As he looks back on the key drivers to their change success, Don says five key actions stand out:

- leadership alignment and accountability
- clear organizational values that resonate
- employee feedback and involvement
- employee alignment and connection
- communication, recognition, and celebration

FEAR AND TRUST

The change process that Don and his company went through took a significant amount of time and energy. It also took a good deal of emotional energy, and this isn't something you can get from a book or from simply working harder and longer. Don's ability to navigate the kind of change they were dealing with had to come from something bigger than Don himself. Don's personal story sheds some light on this.

As a child, Don had an incredible sense of inadequacy. He was afraid to try things because he was sure he was going to fail. Don had really loving, nurturing parents, but for some reason, he was insecure and afraid. He was afraid of going to school. He was afraid of what he was going to be asked to do in class. Many people have similar feelings growing up, but most people outgrow it. Don didn't. In fact, it actually got worse as he got older.

After university, Don decided he wanted to be a Certified Professional Accountant. The process goes like this: for every 100 people that go to the School of Accountancy, 66 pass and write the final exams in the fall (3 days, 4 hours a day). From that number, only 33 receive their designation. For every 100 that start, only 33 are ultimately successful.

For a guy who had a fear of failure, this was probably not a good route to take. But Don took it anyway and began to move through the process. The tension continued to build as the anticipation of the exams drew closer. In fact, for one and a half months before the exams, he was paid by his firm to stay home. He was studying eight or nine hours a day, seven days a week, preparing for the exams that would decide his future career.

At this point in Don's story, it is important to know a little more context about his family. Don grew up in a home where he had a mom and dad who believed in God. Don's parents were more than just "religious" churchgoers; they had a personal relationship with God because of Jesus Christ in their lives. Don saw how this was lived out, and he observed that their relationship with Jesus was something very real and transformative.

As Don became a teenager, he came to a point where it wasn't just his parents' faith; he believed it for himself. Don says, "I understood who God was, and I understood that God loved me so much that he would send his Son, the Lord Jesus, to die for me."

Years before Don led his company through their its "change or die moment," he experienced a similar moment in his personal life. Don was getting ready to take his CPA exams. The morning of the first exam, he was in the shower, and the fear was so overwhelming he found himself unable to move.

Don recalls, "I remember . . . the fear was not just about failing these exams. It was the fear that life would be over if I couldn't do this, I was not good enough, I couldn't make it. I remember just saying, 'God, I can't live this way anymore.'"

Don says there was not a big, booming voice that answered. But in his heart, there was a voice that said, *You don't have to.*

All the things that Don had learned from his parents about God had been head knowledge up until that point. But all of a sudden, all the things that Don knew in his head went down to his heart, and what he heard in his heart was, *God loves you just the way you are. These exams, whether you pass them or fail them, do not define who you are.*

Don passed the exams, and many years later, he led Carswell through a grueling change process. This was possible, in part, because of what he learned that morning in the shower. It wasn't because Don was smarter than the average leader. It was because he had this fundamental sense that no matter what he did in business, it didn't change who he was. God loved Don for who he was. This meant when he failed (and he did fail a few times, as all leaders do), it didn't change how God saw him. But equally important, when Don had success in business, that didn't define him either.

Don reflects on his career, "This is what I did, this was not who I was."

Don's experience in leading change is significant for several reasons. There are certainly lessons and takeaways from his experiences at Carswell. His story illustrates the importance of clearly identifying the why of change and communicating that with everyone involved. It illustrates the challenge of initiating change when things seem to be going well but you know trouble is coming. Don also calls us to courage amidst opposition to change.

Finally, Don reveals his big secret, by letting us in on his personal and spiritual background and the context in which he found the strength to lead. Each of us is on a spiritual journey. None of us has arrived at our ultimate spiritual destination. At some point, we all will face challenges and find out just how strong we are. Don's revelation was that his leadership ability is determined by where he puts his trust. We each have that choice on a daily basis. Either we can trust in our own abilities, intelligence, and determination, or we can use all these while trusting in God, who loves us no matter how successful we are.

LEARNING FROM ELEPHANTS

One of my most memorable life experiences was getting to ride an elephant near Pattaya, Thailand.

My elephant was gently carrying us down a jungle path, yet I also knew this majestic animal had the power to tear down trees and chase down humans. As serene as my experience was, the reality is that no matter how well trained, if the elephant decided it wanted to head in another direction, we would have been pretty powerless to stop it.

And that is where it reminded me of leadership in a large organization.[14] In Don Van Meer's case, the organization in which he was leading had a "way of doing things," and it took some pretty fierce determination to bring about change.

If you want to read more on leading change, one of my favorite books on change leadership is *Switch* by Chip and Dan Heath.[15] In this excellent book, Chip and Dan spell out what I have found to be one of the simplest, but also the most effective, change model I have seen. And not only that—it's about leading an elephant! In their book, Chip and Dan detail examples from many companies and organizations that have sought to bring change successfully.

Large organizations are a little like elephants. They can become big and powerful and deliver strong results over a long period of time, but they can also be difficult to turn around or steer in a new direction.

As Don's story illustrates, leading change is a massive job. Don talks about "get it, feel it, want it" as a way of leading change. Chip and Dan use a similar approach to that which is described by Don in this chapter, with a few differences. In order to steer an elephant, they suggest three steps:

- **Direct the Rider.** The rider sits on top of the elephant, steering it in the direction they want it to go. The rider represents the "rational mind," the more cognitive side of leadership. The use of facts, information, and rational thinking can direct organizations toward change.

- **Motivate the Elephant.** The bulk of the elephant represents the "emotional mind." The basic instincts and reactions of the elephant can at anytime override other factors, and the elephant can move off in whatever direction it wants. It often takes emotionally compelling reasons for people and organizations to change. The elephant must "want" to go in the direction of choice.

- **Shape the Path**. Even if the elephant is being steered in a direction that it wants to go, if the path is uphill, unstable, or unappealing, the elephant may decide to not go in that direction. Leading change also requires clearing obstacles, providing a clear pathway, and making the path more "downhill."

* * *

Questions for Discussion:

1. Think about a change process in which you have been involved. What went well? What didn't go well? Can you say why?

2. What stood out to you from Don's story of change at his company?

3. Is change hard or easy for you? Can you identify anything in your life story that determines your capacity for embracing or leading change?

4. Each of us is on a spiritual journey. Where are you?

4
LET'S TALK

> *Daring leaders say the unsaid, ... and bring to light the stuff that's in the shadows and in the corners.*
>
> —*Brené Brown*[16]

DISCOMFORT

Rowena Yiu was avoiding the issue. She had a colleague whose attitude and behavior made her feel pressured and uncomfortable. It was a bit hard to identify what went wrong, because the woman wasn't doing anything overtly rude. But the feeling that something was "off" in the relationship was growing inside Rowena. And the longer she put off talking about it, the worse it got. We have all had these relationships. Sometimes it's at work, sometimes it's at home with our spouse or kids; but whatever the context, it is unsettling at best. Rowena describes her situation.

"My discomfort built up increasingly, and I started to assume why she did what she did. As time went by, I had this thing growing inside me, even though we had no external conflict. There was a time I was really afraid to see her in person and work closely together."

So Rowena talked with her. In a culture where it was not very common to have revealing conversations, Rowena was going against her own instincts, but she put that aside in order to be honest and then truly listen. She discovered that her assumptions were wrong, that she misunderstood some clues, and that, from the other person's perspective, there was no issue at all. While Rowena was keeping these assumptions inside her, she was trapped in something that wasn't even real. Of course, it was real to Rowena, but it took this crucial conversation to set her free from her own assumptions.

CRUCIAL CONVERSATIONS

As a professional coach, Rowena has conversations with leaders every day. She makes the distinction between consulting and coaching, explaining that while consultants give advice, coaches listen and ask questions to help the clients move forward. What makes some conversations hard is that we simply don't know what the other person is thinking. Rowena has learned to observe, be curious, and continually seek clarity. She has become a learned master in the art of crucial conversations—a conversation in which there may be tension, but the goal is to resolve an issue of importance.

Developing the skill of having crucial conversations is a must for a leader of impact, because these crucial conversations shape our integrated life. They move us forward in our personal relationships, and they offer us an avenue for professional development. Crucial conversations are also an invitation to a deeper spiritual understanding of ourselves and others. Not every conversation is crucial. But it is the crucial conversations that help us to articulate our own thoughts and needs while learning to appreciate and value the needs, opinions, and views of others. Crucial conversations call for our integrity. They also solicit and encourage our growth.

Now, I must personally confess that having crucial conversations is not a strong point for me as a leader, so I am glad to hear Rowena's input. Like Rowena, I come from a culture that tends to avoid conflict. We tend to let things slide . . . slide under the carpet, until they finally trip us up and we have to deal with them.

Some have suggested that this might be because we live in a small set of islands and we feel the need to stay on good terms with everyone, not rock the boat, as there's no place to hide. But the reality is that avoiding these things doesn't tend to make them any better; they just tend to build up.

In New Zealand, we are also not very "direct." As I have worked with North Americans, I learned they can tend to be much more direct. As I was leading a team with many people from the United States, I saw that they would not tend to take my "suggestions" as the "directions" I had intended them to be. I had to learn to be much more direct and communicate in a clearer language, which was uncomfortable for me coming from my cultural context.

WELCOMING SPACE

Another hurdle in communication, besides cultural challenges, is simply time. When people feel we are too busy for them, they hesitate to assert their need for our time. We all have the same amount of time each and every day. Choosing to spend that time with someone in conversation is offering them a gift. Being available, even when we are busy, takes discipline for busy leaders, but the benefits are huge.

This doesn't mean we cannot carve out time for ourselves to be alone and focus. It means that when someone approaches us with a need, we are open, even if we have to say, "Honestly, I'm in the middle of something right now, but I want to find the best time to give you my undivided attention. Can you give me thirty minutes to finish this up?"

Rowena calls this *creating welcoming space.*

Finding time for others is more than responding though. Finding time also means initiating with others. As leaders, we probably have lists, at least in our heads, of people with whom we should stay connected. Taking the initiative with those on our lists takes effort. Building the habit of checking in with our colleagues or family members on a consistent basis is a good way to head off trouble. Many busy leaders have heard, perhaps from their spouse, "We need to talk." If these words cause you discomfort, you probably haven't been taking the time to initiate meaningful conversations. People don't usually start with "we need to talk" when they want to tell you how wonderful you are.

GETTING TO THE REAL ISSUE

In Rowena's conversation with her colleague, she discovered that the real issue was not at all what she assumed. This took intentionality on Rowena's part to communicate because the other person didn't see the problem. So how do you get to the issue? Basically, you let people talk. Asking clarifying questions will help, but people will generally reveal their issue if you are a patient and an active listener.

Here is an example. Let's say you have an employee who is underperforming. There may be any number of reasons for that. Perhaps he is unaware of your standards, or maybe he is lacking a critical skill for the job. Or maybe things aren't going well at home and he is very distracted from his work.

A simple question like, "How do you feel your work is going?" is a good place to start. If we start the conversation with a challenge, such as, "You are really dragging us down. You need to do better," there really is no conversation, and you will have a hard time getting to the real issue.

Asking a question that is open and inviting creates a safe space for the person to respond, and you are, therefore, more likely to get to the root issue. Asking good questions doesn't mean you are avoiding the issue by being indirect. It shows a true interest in the other person. In fact, one consultant called this approach being "ask assertive."

Sometimes the person with whom you are having this talk will act like nothing is wrong. Either he really doesn't know or he is trying to put on a confident facade. Telling him your observations about the results of his work is important. Expressing your concern for him as a valued employee will help disarm him and pave the way toward revealing the real issue.

One of the problems that Rowena encountered was the issue of making assumptions. She assumed some things about her colleague that were wrong. There is a term for this tendency to build up things in our mind that are not true. The term is *vain imaginations*, and it means "a furtive thought that lingers on your mind and begins to wear a rut, repeating itself time and again."[17]

If we tell ourselves, over and over, that someone is not trustworthy, we can convince ourselves that it is true. It takes a crucial conversation to bring the truth to light. Whether we were right or wrong in our assessment, it is better to know the truth.

LISTENING

The Bible also has a lot to say about listening. James 1:19 says,

> My dear brothers and sisters, take note of this: Everyone should be quick to listen, slow to speak and slow to become angry.

This is really good advice. Rowena says, "After I ask a question in a group, I will not be the first person to answer, because I want people to know I value their opinion more than my own. I think this intentionality creates an environment for crucial conversations."

This also applies to one-on-one conversations, in that it is a good practice to ask a question and wait in silence for the answer. What you are communicating is, "I really care about your thoughts."

Rowena mentioned two conversation killers: not listening and making assumptions. This principle also applies in reverse. One leader I know was having a conversation with his boss.

He brought up a topic, and the boss said, "Yes, I know how you feel about that."

Rather than allowing this to kill the conversation, the leader said, "Yes, I know you think you know my perspective. But I would like the chance to state my position again and be sure you really hear me."

The supervisor, to his credit, responded well, sat back, and listened with an open mind.

SPEAK TRUTH AND GRACE

As we consider effective communication, integrated leaders will seek wisdom from the spiritual side of life. For example, when it comes time to give your perspective in a crucial conversation, there are two important concepts to remember: *truth* and *grace*. Truth and grace are, again, tied to principles from the Bible.

Proverbs 3:3 says,

> Let love and faithfulness never leave you; bind them around your neck, write them on the tablet of your heart.

Kindness, or grace, without truth is like flattery. It may make the other person feel better, but it won't really help them. Truth without kindness can be brutal and make it hard for the person to hear the truth.

In a crucial conversation, it is important to remember this principle. In effect, we are saying, "I care enough about you as a person, family member, or valued employee, to tell you the truth."

END WELL AND FOLLOW UP

Sometimes we feel that once we have had a conversation, good communication has taken place. And we have all had the experience of hearing later on that the other party didn't get what we were trying to communicate at all. Asking at the end of the conversation what the person heard you say is a good way to ensure clarity.

You might say, for example, "I really appreciate being able to have this frank and honest conversation with you. I want to make sure you heard me and that I really got the points you were making. Can you share with me what you heard me say?" You can then follow that up with either affirmation or further clarification if needed.

Finally, following up the conversation with appreciation will further reinforce your intention and honor the person's time. You might say, "Hey, I really appreciate the conversation we had yesterday. On further reflection, did anything else occur to you that you want me to know?"

Good leaders have hard conversations. Great leaders initiate crucial conversations, making it a point to preserve the relationship and show respect to the other party.

DON'T WORRY

Of course, just because we feel we have done everything we can to communicate well, there is still no guarantee that the other person will completely understand what we are saying, agree with what we are saying, or respond the way we hope they would.

I recently had a situation where I wanted to give someone some feedback. I gave the feedback in writing, which might have been a mistake! But I did so mostly because I did not feel that the person was hearing me in our personal conversations, and I felt I needed to be concise and clear. It was important to me to be sure that they understood my feedback. Whether they accepted my feedback or agreed with me was not up to me.

We will not always get it perfectly. If, like Rowena and I, you aren't naturally good at this, or it feels countercultural—that's okay! Don't worry about being perfect. The important thing is to be brave, be intentional, and just start the conversation.

* * *

Questions for Discussion:

1. Can you describe a situation where you were avoiding a crucial conversation with someone? What happened?

2. If this is not an area of strength for you, what is one thing you could do differently?

3. Where might you be not "hearing" what someone else is trying to communicate with you? What can you do about it?

5

SUCCESS

Success is no accident. It is hard work, perseverance, learning, studying, sacrifice and most of all, love of what you are doing or learning to do.

—*Pele*[18]

Henry Tan wasn't always successful. An accountant by trade, but an entrepreneur at heart, he dreamed of one day creating and leading a public accounting firm. He cut his teeth at one of the Big Four accounting firms and then started his own business in 1993.

They were small beginnings, opening with just three employees—himself, one partner, and one staff member. To start, they also just needed one client. As Henry shares, "Most of the time, we found that when you do very good work for a client, they tend to recommend you to someone else."

One by one, client by client, the firm continued to grow.

MOMENTUM

Building momentum took time, patience, and energy. It also meant that Henry was taking no salary. Any money generated by the company went back into providing for the company. To provide for his family, Henry taught night classes on finance at a local university and at training schools. He would work from nine to five, grab a small bite to eat along the way, and continue so that he could begin his teaching at seven. He would be home each night around ten thirty, just shy of the start of another long day.

Henry credits his endurance during those early years to the unwavering support of his family. Henry's wife continued working. She and their two sons sacrificed quality time with him while lovingly pushing Henry's dream forward. When Henry was not working or teaching, he prioritized all available time to be with his family. They regularly connected through a nightly family devotional from the Bible. Throughout this stretching season, Henry and his family willingly lived in the tension of ambition. The journey to success is rarely an independent venture.

Today, Henry is the Group CEO of CLA Global TS (formerly Nexia TS), a leading mid-tier public accounting firm in Singapore that offers a full suite of accounting and auditing services. What started with three employees now has over three hundred, with offices in four different countries. CLA Global TS has established itself as an industry leader with international reach. For Henry, it is quite literally a dream come true.

"BE NICE"

Henry was initially hesitant to discuss his professional success. The word *success* can have negative connotations, mainly because everyone defines success differently. It is less of a finish line and more of a moving target. For Henry, success is not actually measured by company productivity or individual recognition. Henry said that success for him is "knowing what my purpose in life is."

As a follower of Jesus, Henry has found his greatest expression of purpose in loving God and, in turn, loving others and showing compassion toward them. For him, that starts in his home—that his wife and sons would feel loved, supported, and encouraged. But this compassion also overflows into his professional life.

Part of his business acumen is to have an empathetic lens for others—to see them as people first, employees and clients second. They are real people with real lives, real struggles, and real needs.

Henry says, "Talking to one of my team members, and they have a situation where one spouse was stuck in another country and this young mom is taking care of her children and trying to work. And despite this, she's still putting in a lot of effort and working very hard. So if we, as leaders, are able to be human and to show love and compassion, the same love and compassion that was first shown to us, that makes a big difference."

So when asked what Henry considers to be his secret to success, his reply is short and succinct: "Be nice."

The word *nice* for Henry carries more weight than the simplicity of his response implies. It has shaped the way he sees, pursues, and leads those within his organization. At CLA Global TS, this has created a culture of investment and engagement that permeates throughout—from their CEO, to their employees, which is then forwarded to the clients they serve.

INTEGRATED AUTHENTICITY

Being nice, though, is only as meaningful as it is genuine. That is why living an integrated life is so important to Henry.

As Henry says, "An integrated life involves the personal, professional, and spiritual. For the personal side, that is my family. I need to be a role model for my children. For the professional side, I'm the CEO of the group. I need to be a role model for all of the employees, the staff, and my partners who are working at that level. People are looking to me for consistent behavior. That is not from my own strength, it comes from God, and it is a natural expression of my identity in him."

Within his organization, this expression of authenticity and integration is fostered by reliability on core values. At CLA Global TS, they seek to "listen, think, steer, innovate, and grow to be a strategist for Asia." Listening allows them to understand the needs of their clients.

As Henry says, "Wisdom is found in listening."

Thinking allows them the space to consider the issues at hand and move forward with real, meaningful solutions. And growing pushes them to intentionally invest their impact and contribute to society in the businesses and places that they are planted in as an organization. Undergirding these corporate values are the twin pillars of integrity and respect for others.

Henry shares, "In terms of our nature of work in auditing, accounting, and consulting, it is so important for our clients to know that whatever we say to them is true. And in turn, we expect truth from our clients. We also want to have mutual respect at all levels. Even if a junior person really fouls up their work . . . No one dresses themselves up, combs their hair, and comes to the workplace just to try to mess things up. If someone fails, respect that person. They are more than that mistake."

Within his company, that mutual respect is not a free pass for underperformance, but it is instead an invitation for each person to treat others as they would like to be treated. In creating a culture of understanding and respect, Henry has also fostered loyalty and a deep investment from those most responsible for his success—his employees and clients.

Henry's firm has defined who they are: "We come to work every day with a singular purpose—to create winning opportunities for our people, our clients, and our communities."

MEASURE OF SUCCESS

The true measure of success is often forged in fire. And for Henry, the proverbial fire came with the Covid-19 pandemic. Like many marketplace leaders, he was thrust into a new, ever-changing situation with the burden and mantle of leadership to carry.

In a pre-pandemic context, CLA Global TS required their auditors to go directly to the client's place of business. With lockdowns and restrictions, it became clear that COVID would greatly affect the daily operations of the organization. Henry was deeply troubled.

How would they carry out their work? How would they invoice and bill the clients? How would they pay the staff and the other expenses to run the business?

Henry describes those days, saying, "I was at a loss at the time. And I couldn't sleep really well. And so, I woke up very early. I decided to take a walk. And as I walked, I began to feel that there just seems to be something speaking to me. So as I walked, I basically pulled out all the concerns I have. Should I do this? Should I do that? And what if I did this and it didn't work out? And during this walk, I just had this sort of sense that there is something prompting me to say the word *sacrifice*.

"So when I went back to my office, I decided to make an announcement to all my directors and partners to say, 'I think that in order for us to weather this, I, personally, as group CEO, would like to take a 30 percent salary reduction to reduce the costs of the company.' And I invited all my partners to see if they were willing to also make a sacrifice. Most of the staff also joined together with us to take a 20 percent pay cut. At that point, the cash reserves could last us two to three months, but we were actually able to build up to six to eight months of reserve. Surprisingly, after we had done this, and everyone agreed to it, the business did not decline. We adapted. We managed to work and collect in various ways. And in the end, we were able to return a bonus to everyone who made the sacrifice."

Henry and his team had weathered the storm.

He is humble in the retelling. He chose to sacrifice his own pay for employee retention. And his employees, in turn, chose to sacrifice because they knew the faithful character of their leader. Henry's success wasn't defined by making it through the pandemic. The situation merely highlighted what had been true of Henry's leadership all along—his values for authenticity, integrity, and being nice have consistently permeated the culture of his organization. But Henry's values, and the success they have brought, have a much deeper root.

For Henry, that still, small voice he heard on his walk in March 2020 was not just something conjured from inside himself. He had heard that voice many times before on his journey up the corporate ladder. Living an integrated, Spirit-filled life, Henry knew to whom the voice belonged—it was God's. Henry's relationship with God has continually acted as his "compass." And being deeply rooted in that relationship has always given him the faith and boldness to step into his purpose.

And for Henry, knowing his purpose is the measure of success that keeps driving him, and his organization, forward.

CULTURE

Our cultural background can also have a great impact on the way we view and treat success. Henry is a very successful leader, yet he also comes across as incredibly humble. I have found this trait to be true of many leaders I have met from Asian cultures.

I come from a small country in the South Pacific, New Zealand, but I recently spent six years working in the United States, and the approach to success and recognition of that success really stood out to me.

In New Zealand, we talk about something called the "tall poppy syndrome." Essentially, this means that if one poppy appears to be so much taller than others, you need to cut it down to size. Translated into leadership situations, often success can be seen as negative by others; to rise above others goes against the more egalitarian values of our society. This can result in wrongly attributed negative perceptions of business leaders who are successful, often with an assumption that they may have achieved their success at the cost of others. New Zealanders have a tendency to back the underdog more than the obviously competent. We have got a way to go in recognizing that success can be a result of doing good things really well.

By contrast, in the United States, I observed that it is usually seen as a positive thing to be successful; it's part of the American dream! Success can even serve as a source of inspiration for others. While leading a large global team from the United States, I found that my New Zealand approach meant that I was often underreporting the work of my team. While it went against my cultural tendency to downplay success, I learned that I needed to be a more vocal and stronger spokesperson for our success. Often, practical things like funding and staffing depended on being good at telling success stories. I found that Americans tended to back winners, not the underdogs.

These are, of course, just my observations, but as leaders, it can be important to evaluate cultural responses to success and the assumptions we make, consciously or unconsciously.

Leaders like Henry help me see that success and humility can go together, and they can inspire us toward success that makes a positive impact in the world around us.

VALUES

Henry's personal values greatly impact his role as leader. For Henry, his values have been determined by his relationship with God, have been learned through his study of the Bible, and then applied to his personal and professional life. In fact, all our values greatly influence all we do and say, and it can be more a matter of whether we are conscious of this or not. Becoming more conscious of our values and being able to articulate them can really help us grow as leaders.

LeaderImpact has a course called "Foundations," which includes a look at our core values and how they shape our leadership.[19]

* * *

Questions for Discussion:

1. How do you define success? Does "be nice" resonate with you?
2. What would you say is your secret to success?
3. What core values contribute to your success? And why do you have those values?
4. How is success viewed in your culture? How does that affect your drive to succeed as a leader?

6

MONEY, MONEY, MONEY

It's a rich man's world.

—*Abba*[20]

WALKING AWAY

Enoch Weng grew up in a family of artists. The family has an art institute in Vancouver, Canada, and Enoch was on a path to be a jazz musician. Because his family specializes in helping students get into prestigious art schools and schools of music, to Enoch this seemed a natural path. Then Enoch's life took a strange turn. He applied for university and was accepted into business school. His friends were excited for him. His family was totally supportive. And Enoch was confused.

It was definitely not easy. The first few years, Enoch actually absolutely disliked the business world. It seemed as though Enoch was there to make friends, but everybody else was focused on business. He struggled with the concepts of making rich people richer and wanted to do good for people. This led him to the nonprofit world.

Enoch loved the nonprofit world. He just hated the fact that there was no money. The irony was inescapable. In the for-profit sector, there was greed with all the abundance and too much focus on money. In the nonprofit world, there was scarcity and, therefore, also too much focus on money. This led Enoch to think, *Okay then, where can I make money so I can help these people?* And that led to tech.

Enoch's tech world experience was all about start-ups, scaling, and business training and market validation, and he loved it. He was seeing success in his career and making money. And then he felt God asking him to step away from it.

Enoch remembers, "It was at that moment when God kind of tugs at your heart and knocks at your door. And then I heard God say, 'Hey, I'm calling you out. You need to leave your job.' And I think, 'Leave my job? Leave this career? And I'm, like, no God, I just got here.' I was just so confused. But I let my contract go and walked away."

Imagine the feeling. Enoch knew he had to walk away from his career, and he knew there must be a pretty good reason. He just didn't know why.

The initial excitement of walking away from a career to pursue something unknown waned after a period of time because God seemed silent. The days turned into months, and Enoch became increasingly frustrated as he watched his bank account drop while many of his friends were moving on with life. They were gaining promotions and getting married, while Enoch felt angry and stuck.

He wrestled with God through this difficult time. But it was also a time where he began to understand himself in new ways. A time when he discovered that he had built his identity and self-worth on titles, achievements, and wealth. For the first time, Enoch gave up all these things to seek the Lord. It was then that he first began to realize that his faith and his work needed to be reconciled. And that was the moment when his life completely changed and things began to open up.

We all have a story. Enoch's story tells the background and context of his life and the integration of his personal, professional, and spiritual lives. Understanding our story involves asking questions like, "What keeps you up at night?" and "What are you passionate about?"

RISING ABOVE

The context of Enoch's life experiences led him to start a company called Rise Above Finance, helping people realign their finances with biblical values and principles. People come to them with money problems or goals like home ownership or a retirement plan. While the advice Enoch's team gives is practical, inevitably, the conversation turns to the client's story. What are the things that keep them up at night? What are the things that make them pound the table? These different themes make up their story and give Enoch and his team the clues to be a part of their journey, helping to guide them and shape their future.

This reminds me of Jesus's words:

> For where your treasure is, there your heart will be also.[21]

Finance seems very tangible. It is so much easier to quantify than things like change or stress management. But how we handle our finances has a tremendous impact on how we live our lives personally, professionally, and spiritually. There are a lot of great resources on finance from a biblical perspective, but this book is about how to live the integrated life of a leader, and this chapter is about how to put our finances in the context of that integrated life. Money is not just a practical and pragmatic part of our lives; it affects all of us. It impacts the integrated life by influencing the personal, professional, and spiritual.

OWNERSHIP

There is a big difference in how we view our own money versus other people's money. If we are talking about saving, spending, earning, or investing our own money, we tend to be very interested and much more careful. We are much more thoughtful with money we worked hard for. We can also feel that since we worked hard for that money, we are entitled to spend it any way that we want.

There is, however, a principle from the Bible that challenges our concept of ownership. Psalm 24:1 says,

> The earth is the Lord's, and everything in it, the world, and all who live in it.

So if God made the world and it all ultimately belongs to him, then what is our role? For those who are followers of Christ, we must consider that if everything belongs to God the Creator, then we are not ultimately the owners. The Bible goes on to explain that God made man to "rule over" the earth, or to be "stewards" of it. This is where we get the concept of stewardship.

STEWARDSHIP

Stewardship requires taking responsibility for something entrusted to us.

There is also a great story in the Bible about a wealthy property owner. He decided to go on a trip and called in three of his key employees, giving them stewardship over a certain amount of money. To one, he gave five talents, to another he gave two, and to the third, he gave one talent. (A talent was a measure of money, and it was a significant amount. A talent was worth twenty years' wages for a common laborer.)

The three employees then took the money and, as stewards, had to decide what to do with the money that was entrusted to them. You can read Matthew 25:14–30 for the complete story and note especially the response of the owner to each of them. Essentially, this story illustrates that Jesus has a very high expectation of performance for people entrusted with his resources.

He rewarded those who did well and punished those who were lazy.

Stewardship demands that we take the management of what is entrusted to us seriously. Whether we have a lot or a little in terms of money and possessions is not the point. Knowing who is the ultimate owner and knowing and understanding our role as stewards is critical. Being a good steward means that we should stop and ask the owner (God), "What do you want me to do with your money?"

INTEGRATED LIFE

The integrated life is built on the concept that everything in our lives is interconnected. While this makes sense in a grand way, we still tend to compartmentalize our lives. We think, erroneously, that we leave work and go home then some switch clicks and we can be a different person. But it really doesn't work that way. Whether we are at work, at home, at our place of worship, or on vacation, the common denominator is us. We take ourselves, with all our joys and struggles and unsolved problems, wherever we go.

Because money as a concept is all-pervading, we take our ideas about money and finance to work, and then we take them home at the end of our day. If we are generous at home, we will tend to be generous at work. If we view ourselves as stewards of what God has given us, when we are at work, we will let our spiritual values guide our decisions about corporate finance. And we will make decisions on things like lifestyle and gifts for our children and how much to save for retirement based on our beliefs.

Here is a question for you:

What do you think is God's purpose for your money and finance?

How you answer that question will do two things for you. First, it will reveal what your values are and shed some light on your past. Second, it will shape your future. Literally.

Enoch's answer to this important question of purpose is, "God blesses us so we can bless others."

4 RS

Enoch's team has built a whole business on helping their clients figure out what that purpose means for them.[22] They think of finance in terms of four *R*s: relationship, repent, reframe, and respond. While this is a framework that applies to all areas of life, it works especially well in finance.

A simple way to look at the four *R*s is to ask questions that will lead us to apply the concepts in our own life.

- **Relationship.** What is our relationship with God, and how does this affect our stewardship of what he has given us? Are there things we need to do to strengthen our trust in him? What would he have us do in order to bless others as we have been blessed?

- **Repent.** Where do I need to change my attitude or actions? (*Repent* literally means "to change your mind about something.") Do I seek first the kingdom of God with my finances? As God shows us areas where we have had wrong attitudes, turning from those attitudes and developing a biblical view will help us get on track.

- **Reframe.** In what areas do I need to take another look? What does God's Word say about money and money management? How will my new perspective shape my budget? What are some biblical principles that can guide me with my decision-making?

- **Respond.** What can I do in the next ninety days to effectively act as a better steward of what God has entrusted to me?

PAYOFF

Finally, the big payoff! Generosity!

Dave Ramsey, a well-known author on finance, tells a great story about a class in which several couples were learning biblical principles of finance. One of the couples was a young family, and when asked what their motivation was for getting their finances in order, they confided that they wanted to get completely out of debt so they could afford to adopt another child. They had already made significant progress and had only $15,000 of debt left.

An older couple who happened to be at their table called them that evening and asked if they could come over for a quick visit. The couple agreed, and when the older couple arrived and sat down, they told them they had been employing the principles in the class to their own finances for several years and were looking for where God wanted them to bless others. They were touched by the story of this young couple, paid off their remaining debt, and left the meeting with a huge smile on their faces.

Which couple enjoyed that interaction more? Hard to say. That is what happens when leaders have a positive impact on the lives of others.[23]

POSITIVE IMPACT

Some of us are entrusted with a lot of money, and some with little. The amount is not necessarily the issue; it's what we do with it.

As leaders seeking to live an integrated life, we desire to have a positive impact on the lives of those around us and on our communities, cities, and countries. Utilizing our financial resources, large or small, for positive impact is a significant part of a well-integrated life.

One of the great examples who impacted me growing up was a man called Robert Laidlaw. He started one of the largest retail companies in New Zealand, the Farmers Trading Company. Begun in 1909 largely as a mail-order business, it grew into a department store, then multiple retail stores nationwide, and now online. It remains one of the most-trusted businesses in our country. But what most people don't know is that the founder held a strong Christian faith and was one of the greatest philanthropists of his time in our nation. He remarked that the more be gave, the more he was blessed with, reflecting what it says in the Bible:

> Remember this: Whoever sows sparingly will also reap sparingly, and whoever sows generously will also reap generously.[24]

* * *

Questions for Discussion:

1. If you looked at your bank or credit card statement for the past month, would it reflect your values? If so, in what ways?

2. Have you experienced the principle of "sowing and reaping"—the more generous you are, the more you have to share?

3. What challenges you most about Enoch's story and perspective on finances?

7

RISKY BUSINESS

Someone is sitting in the shade today because someone planted a tree a long time ago.

—*Warren Buffett*[25]

PURPOSEFUL RISK-TAKING

Garth Jestley knows a lot about risk.[26] As the senior leader and CEO of an investment management business, Garth had the opportunity to invest in his firm but needed to borrow millions of dollars from the bank to pay for the shares. The short story—he seized the opportunity and was rewarded with a great return on investment over the years he held it, through dividend payments and ultimately the sale of his interest to his partners in 2012. The longer story illustrates how leaders assess, put in context, and, ultimately, take risks. Garth calls this "taking risk on purpose."

Risk is inevitable. Sometimes it comes in the form of opportunities that we unearth or are offered. Sometimes risk is thrust upon us by factors beyond our control.

Risk is a fundamental fact of life.

A simple definition of *risk* is "the uncertainty that surrounds the outcome of any activity." When you know that a restaurant has served you reasonable food at a good price for years, taking someone important to dinner there is low risk. On the other hand, a new place you know nothing about carries a higher risk. Obviously, financial investments or hiring key employees are inherently riskier activities, but the principles are the same. Whatever you decide, the point is that you take the risk, on purpose, and that process is what makes you an intelligent risk-taker.

After a long career in the investment business—including venture capital, private equity, and the creation and management of pooled funds that invest in publicly traded companies—Garth Jestley has a lot of wisdom on taking risks, and this chapter seeks to draw out some of his insights.

One of the principal lessons Garth says he has learned from the investment profession is that taking risks is good provided one takes it on purpose.

"Taking risk is good because it is the gateway to reward. In other words, no risk equals no return. Or, quoting author Stephen Covey, 'The greatest risk is the risk of riskless living.'"[27]

According to Jestley, taking risk "on purpose" implies that the potential reward is commensurate with the risk taken. It also implies that one is able to identify the risk and analyze it intelligently. The assessment of potential reward and risk, taken together, translates into calculated, or purposeful, risk-taking.

David Packard, of Hewlett Packard fame, said, "Take risks. Ask big questions. Don't be afraid to make mistakes; if you don't make mistakes, you're not reaching far enough."[28]

A leader of impact can't afford to just play it safe. At the same time, risks should be taken intentionally and intelligently.

RISK AND PEOPLE

One of Garth Jestley's key lessons has to do with the "people" side of risk. Taking risks on people is fraught with danger and yet has the potential to yield huge rewards. Leaders of impact know that we don't get very far if we have to be in control of everything. Finding and consulting with people we trust is part of a robust risk assessment process. We all know the value of seeking out an intelligent person as a sounding board. Talking things over with our spouse or a good friend who has our best interest at heart can help us be more objective and a lot more successful than when we don't consult others.

The people side of risk is also inevitable. When we are deciding whether to invest in a company, we must carefully assess the values and know the track record of its leader. When we are deciding whether to marry someone, we want to know his or her character, family background, and interests. We have all taken many risks in our lives. And since the outcomes are uncertain, we have all experienced the joy of reward in some cases and the pain of loss or heartbreak in others.

Let's be a little more specific. Say you are deciding whether to invest in a company. The management of that company is critical to the potential success of your investment.

Jestley says, "First, never compromise on the issue of integrity. If someone lies once, assume that they always lie, and on this basis alone, do not invest."

When someone gives you references, do not solely rely on those references, but instead do due diligence calls to those with no known loyalty to that person. According to Jestley, "This is one of the best ways to uncover character and competence problems."

When considering whether to invest in a new company, understanding the entrepreneur's motivation and character are critical. Here are some very practical questions to ask:

1. How strongly does the entrepreneur want to succeed?
2. How much money has he or she invested?
3. How hard do they work?
4. Do they really understand that the road ahead will be full of challenges, known and unknown?
5. Are they humble? Do they appreciate that they don't have a monopoly on wisdom?
6. What is their track record of dealing with adversity?
7. Do they remain positive in the face of negative developments?
8. What are their observable values?

A final consideration regarding the person in whom you are considering investing is their respect for risk.

Jestley says, "By their nature, entrepreneurs are optimists. This attitude is critical to success. However, they must temper their optimism with realism and contingency planning. Perhaps surprisingly, great entrepreneurs usually have a healthy degree of risk aversion."

If you look back at the previous list, you can see that it applies to any risk you are considering. Whether you are thinking about getting married, choosing a school for your children, or investing in a company, the same questions apply.

THE INTEGRATED LIFE

A key feature of an integrated life is that of context. Things we do in our personal lives have an impact on our professional and spiritual lives. How we feel about our professional role affects how we conduct ourselves in our personal lives. This all relates to risk-taking in the sense that we take risks in the context of our whole lives. For example, when offered an opportunity to invest in a business venture, we should evaluate the financial potential of the investment in the context of both personal financial exposure and reputational risk.

Important factors in risk assessment include questions like, "Does the business venture have clear goals and strategies that are not in conflict with my own purpose and values?" Many opportunities look good at first glance, but when we realize the company is known for shady business dealings, we should avoid the opportunity.

RISK AND PURPOSE

Another type of risk has to do with where we choose to invest our time and energy.

Garth Jestley remembers starting out in the corporate world full of energy and passion and receiving promotions and responsibilities. What he didn't anticipate was reaching his goals early in his professional career and asking himself fundamental questions like, "What was that all about?" and "What was the purpose of all the striving and stress to become the vice president of Citibank?"

Jestley recalls, "I suddenly realized with great clarity that I would experience the same feelings and questions when I became senior vice president of the bank and beyond as I pursued greater accolades, responsibility, and compensation. Needless to say, these revelations were extremely disconcerting. I knew then that I needed to pursue the question of purpose. There simply had to be something more to life than finding my identity in work and pursuing power and money. I understood that achieving these goals without answering this fundamental question would inevitably be deeply unsatisfying."

It was at this point that Garth was primed for a big change. Whenever we start thinking about the fundamental questions of life, like purpose, we open ourselves up to thinking outside the box. Because he was deeply dissatisfied with his own life despite outward success, Garth agreed to accompany his wife, Mary, to church in his midthirties. He decided there was no risk in being open-minded, and during that service, he began a journey of faith, taking a step to believe in God and trust him with his life.

Garth says, "The question of purpose and destiny, which had caused such angst during my crisis of success, was fully answered when I encountered the person of Jesus Christ. In that moment, God became real to me, and with that revelation came the realization that he is the one who determines my life's purpose. As well, through Jesus's sacrifice on the cross, he is the one who guarantees my destiny. While work remained an important part of my life, it did not consume me any longer. Whereas I had previously often experienced high levels of stress, I now felt a genuine peace in the midst of every business emergency, and they tend to come with some frequency in the investment industry. This included dealing with the inevitable ethical pressures.

"The financial services industry, and particularly the investment business, is among the most highly regulated in the world precisely because of the conflicts of interest and the pressure to not do the right thing for your clients in order to make more money. I now make every effort to do the right thing in every situation. Also, I pray over my business and often receive wisdom as to which course of action I should take. Over the years, we experienced major adversity in our business on occasion, but I always felt God's peace even when others were having great difficulty coping.

"Mary and my children became much more important priorities to me than they had been. While Mary and I had always enjoyed a strong relationship prior to my decision to follow Christ, we were now 'on the same page' in terms of our shared faith. As a result, we became much better at resolving the conflicts that crop up from time to time in all marriages, since we were both united in seeking God's will in every circumstance.

"In summary, I believe that my decision to follow Christ was the best risk I ever took on purpose. It was a risk in the sense that I was relinquishing control over my life to God rather than continuing to live autonomously. That said, I firmly believe that the benefits of trusting God, including finding peace, purpose, and security about my future, far outweigh the risk. In any event, I strongly believe that the much greater risk is to live one's life without reference to God."

Garth says, "Risk-taking in the investment business is a great example of purposeful risk-taking. However, it pales by comparison with the ultimate example: the risk Jesus Christ took on purpose for the reward of reconciling humankind with God. To quote prolific author Andrew Wommack,

> Most of us would not have created the world and man if we knew the heartache and terrible sacrifice it would cost. But God is not man. In His judgment [which is the correct judgment] the prize was worth the cost.[29]

"In light of God's absolute perfection (including his unequaled power, wisdom, love, and justice), it is both affirming and humbling to know that he valued each one of us so highly (his reward) that our creation and rescue were his top priority. Regarding risk, consider that Jesus chose death on a cross for the joy set before him. According to Psalm 16:10, Jesus took this purposeful risk because he trusted in God the Father to not abandon him to the realm of the dead nor let him see decay."

GET IN THE GAME

As I reflect on Garth's perspective on risk, I am reminded of a time when I was in my early twenties and attended a basketball game after work with some friends. I had come to watch the game straight from my job in the government, so I was still wearing a business suit.

Once the game was over, spectators were allowed to go down to the court and shoot a few hoops if they wanted. I looked at my suit and thought, *No, I don't want to mess up my trousers, so I'll just sit it out while my friends have some fun on the court.* I felt bad about it, but I didn't want to take the risk.

After the game, we left the arena and headed for the car park. It was dark, and as we walked, I tripped on a railing, fell to the ground, and completely ripped my suit trousers! They were beyond repair. And I thought to myself, *I should have just joined in the game!*

This early moment has stuck with me—that when I am offered an opportunity like this, I should just go ahead and get in the game.

Life is full of risks, and as long as they are not life-threatening or reckless, it is better to get fully involved in life rather than hold back.

Taking risks on purpose can lead to a much more fulfilled, enjoyable, fruitful, and integrated life as we consider the personal, professional, and spiritual aspects of any particular decision.

* * *

Questions for Discussion:

1. How would you describe your approach to risk? Does it differ in your personal or spiritual life when compared with your work life?

2. What is the biggest risk you have taken? What did you learn from it?

3. What is one risk you can take this week or year "on purpose"?

8
HONEY, I'M HOME!

If you want to make a positive impact, no matter how far-reaching, start at home. Treat your family members like treasures.

—John Maxwell[30]

Keith and Esther Dindi had a tough decision to make. As a cardiac surgeon in the busiest heart hospital in Kenya, Keith was busy and fulfilled in his profession. Esther, meanwhile, had her own medical practice as an internist and specialist in holistic medicine and wellness. To add to these very demanding careers, the Dindis were blessed with twin teenagers and a third child, a few years younger. Life was full.

Then the call came. An opportunity to get to the cutting edge of technology as a cardiac surgeon was made available to Keith. But it was in Melbourne, Australia. In terms of career path, this was, in Keith's words, a no-brainer. In terms of family dynamics, a prospective move to another continent was daunting. How Keith and Esther made that decision is a study in marriage and family dynamics.

Keith and Esther Dindi were born and raised in Kenya. Keith was quite sick as a child and was in and out of hospitals for surgery and treatments. One might suppose that this would create an aversion to all things medical. In Keith it was the opposite, resulting in a passion for medicine.

Keith and Esther met in medical school. Esther was to become a specialist in internal medicine while Keith went the route of cardiac surgery. Keith describes the first time he saw Esther.

"I first saw her when she was playing basketball, and she had these amazing long legs running along the basketball court. She was smiling and laughing, even when she would miss her shots, and I noticed the happiness and joy that I saw on her face, wherever she was. I just felt she was the kind of person I wanted to spend the rest of my life with."

Medical school is a long haul. Keith and Esther courted for five years, and upon graduation, they married in 2005. In 2008, the twins were born on Esther's birthday.

So here we have a young couple, both in busy careers, with twins, and as if that is not enough, they have discovered a shared entrepreneurial spirit. They have businesses in the area of wellness, and Esther has a brand called Dr. Fitness. They also run a nonprofit organization called Thriving Couples, which helps married couples navigate a successful relationship in the context of a culture that can seem to divide rather than unite.[31]

TWO COMMITMENTS

There are two overriding commitments that Keith and Esther share. One is their commitment to each other. The other is a shared commitment to God and living their lives in a way that honors him. As we each pursue our own spiritual journey, and pursue relationships that really work, it is fascinating to look inside the lives of this couple to find out what makes life work for them.

From a big-picture perspective, the Dindis live life from a sense of purpose. They think of their purpose as using the gifts and talents God has given them to serve humanity. This filter affects decisions—both big decisions, like a move, and also the seemingly inconsequential little decisions that make up our days. From a very practical perspective, the Dindis share what makes life work for them.

INTENTIONALITY

Perhaps the most glaring thing about Keith and Esther's marriage is how much time they commit to each other. It's not surprising to most people that communication is considered to be the key to success in a marriage relationship. Knowing this and putting good communication into practice in today's overcommitted society is another thing. This level of communication takes intentionality, and this requires setting in place some habits that will ensure good communication.

Keith and Esther have a habit of breakfast together, every morning, as a family. This time to start the day, checking in with each other and the children, knowing the potential challenges of each person's day, shows commitment and care. Texting each other and the children during the day keeps that connection alive. Then, each evening, Keith and Esther try to go for a walk together, rehashing the day. This obviously also adds a bit of exercise to the formula.

The Dindis admit that this isn't always easy. During their master's degree training, Keith and Esther were both busy students, with small children, living in a city with all the intensity of a daily commute, when they realized that they had to decide whether their lives were going to be lived together and integrated.

The integrated life that LeaderImpact talks about is not just theory for the Dindis. The natural thing for people who lead challenging busy lives is to compartmentalize. Those who are leading companies in technology, for example, are challenged by the shifting dynamics of an ever-changing market. The temptation is to focus solely on work, letting family and spiritual pursuits fade in importance. We tend to tell ourselves, "It's only for a season. When I get to this next level, I will regain some balance." Oftentimes, balance never comes.

There is a counterintuitive aspect to the integrated life. As leaders, we are used to solving problems. Often, this takes a pretty singular focus. The irony of the integrated life is that it is easier to be successful at home when things are going well at work and vice versa. When we are fulfilled and growing spiritually, we have more to bring to the relationships that are important to us. It seems harder to bring our best selves to work and home at the same time, but this is where true success lies.

As Keith says, "If you're not a hero at home, you can never be the hero in your workplace."

Just because you are saving lives at work doesn't mean you can drop the ball at home.

DEFINING SUCCESS

Keith and Esther are quick to point out that perfection is simply not possible. Esther says, "No one should feel undue pressure when things don't seem harmonious, when things don't seem to be integrated or in balance. You may think you have it right today, but then tomorrow things come up because life is so dynamic."

We can all aspire to progress though. Knowing that things will shift and routines will change depending on the various seasons of life takes some of the pressure off.

Success also means being able to be present. Each of us has experienced talking with someone who seems to be somewhere else. Perhaps you know someone who has the ability to focus on whoever he or she is talking with, making that person feel like the only person on the planet. This is a gift, but it is also a skill that can be cultivated. This takes discipline.

Successful leaders, whether at home or at work, have the ability to focus on the tasks and the people at hand.

Esther shares, "When I am in the workplace, seeing patients and working with my interns, I work toward being present at the moment. I will also be present and mindful when I am with the kids at home."

Keith acknowledges that life is not always pleasant conversations. He talks about how, when in a disagreement, it is important to focus on dealing with an issue and not "dealing with a person." In other words, if you picture yourself and the person you are talking with on one side of a table, and the issue on the other side, you can talk it through without opposing one another. This leads to conversation about resolving the issue, or fixing the problem, rather than fixing the person.

A FAMILY DECISION

Let's go back to Keith and Esther's decision to move to Australia. This was a great opportunity for Keith. The advancement of his skill as a heart surgeon would end up being useful in serving the people back home as well. But it would mean Esther putting some of her work on pause and moving across the world with children who were just entering high school added as another dynamic. So the Dindis took time to get away and talk, pray, and discuss all the implications of the move. One decision that was already made was that if Keith needed to go, they would go together. Keith and Esther had decided early in their marriage that they never wanted to live apart as a couple.

Esther says, "Keith has gifted hands in the area of heart surgery, and I could see as he talked about these things, he would just be beaming with excitement."

As they began to pursue the opportunity, however, they had the interruption of the global pandemic. This slowed the process down and delayed the move and, inevitably, changed the dynamics of the family as well. As they discussed their priorities—namely, their relationship with God, their marriage, and the kids—they began to see God's provision.

Finally, the decision was made as a family, and the Dindis took the step of faith and moved across the other side of the world. This has meant that some of their family has been apart at times. However, Keith and Esther Dindi grew up in a very communal culture, and they have a supportive network of extended family and friends who have helped them manage this season well.

Esther says, "I would say that all these things don't work the same for different people. And I believe when you have a certain desire and follow-through, God has a way of making other provisions."

What Keith and Esther have shown us is a good marriage. We take heart in their commitment to the life they have together. They live out the principles of integration, communication, focus, and community. Their journey is different from ours. In fact, all our journeys are different. Their commitment to the spiritual dimension of life inspires us to stay true to what we believe in and discover how to know God and his purposes for us. And to do that together.

OUR FAMILY DECISION

In 2013, my family faced a similar decision to the Dindis. I was quietly minding my own business in New Zealand when an opportunity was put before me to apply for a global role for our organization based in Florida, USA. It represented a large promotion for me, with global leadership over our work of about 8,000 staff in over 150 countries. There would be a lot of challenges, travel, and most likely, stress. It would also mean my wonderful wife and two boys, aged fourteen and twelve, would need to uproot their lives and make a life in Florida while I was busy working and traveling the world.

My wife, Nicki, felt ready for the challenge, but we wanted it to be a family decision if I was offered the role. Because of the challenges ahead, we knew that if not all of us were on board, it could make it very difficult when things got tough along the way.

It helped that our family had been on a trip to Florida the year before. So when we talked with our boys about it, for our twelve-year-old, the adventure of living in America with Disney World on your doorstep was pretty attractive! Then my fourteen-year-old summed it up to me, saying, "Dad, if you feel this is what God wants you to do, we should just do it!"

Oh, the faith of the young! But he was right, and we had many factors pointing to this being the right direction, so we agreed as a family to pack up and go. So we sold almost everything and moved to Florida for six years.

It turned out to be a great leadership experience for me, and we saw a lot of growth in our work globally over that time. Our family also had many great experiences both in the United States and around the world as we sometimes got to travel together. I am also sure it was a much better experience for having come together to make the decision as a family.

In fact, after six years, we were beginning to sense it might be time to move back to New Zealand. We had a number of conversations together, and in the end, we concluded as a family that it was time to make the change. After returning to New Zealand, we have kept up with one particular US tradition, that of the Thanksgiving holiday.

We have much to be thankful for as a family, and it is good to pause and remember this.

***

Questions for Discussion:

1. In what ways can you relate to the challenge of being a hero at work and struggling with success at home?

2. Can you think of a decision you have faced that had a big impact on your family? How did you make the decision?

3. Which principle for succeeding at home stands out to you from Keith and Esther's story?

9
BETTER TOGETHER

It's always better when we're together.

—Jack Johnson[32]

Many aspects of leadership can be daunting and difficult and, therefore, easy to procrastinate on. I am very motivated by doing things *with* people. I think I could do almost anything, if it was with the right people!

I have found this to be true in many parts of my life, from exercise to leadership. I was definitely in the best shape of my life when I was regularly going to the gym with a friend who knew what he was doing. And I have enjoyed leading the most when I have had the privilege to work alongside great people! People and community make a difference. Eni Xheko is a good example of a leader making a difference in the context of community.

Eni is a busy woman. After studying marketing and business administration in France and the United States, she returned home to Tirana, Albania, where, since 2009, she has been managing her family business. Her father had opened a 4-star hotel in Tirana in 1993, and currently Eni manages one hundred employees. She also has two children. She is a former board member of the American Chamber of Commerce in Albania and has taught business management at a private university. How does she do all that? The answer is, she doesn't do it all alone. Community is key to a leader.

Having a group of people with whom you share values, struggles, and growth is life-giving. Eni is part of LeaderImpact, where her group discusses how to integrate all they are learning personally, professionally, and spiritually. Even though being a mom, a manager, a board member, and a teacher are quite different roles, Eni is still only one person. Community is where we gain strength and perspective for greater impact.

As you get to know Eni, you discover several principles that make her life work. These principles are all part of living life in a community.

GETTING AND GIVING

As leaders, it is important, even critical, to continue to grow as a person. In a community, we find relationships that pour into our lives. We receive the encouragement, knowledge, and courage to apply what we are learning. We also have the opportunity to give that same encouragement and knowledge to others.

Eni says, "I've always wanted to be with people who have a bigger plate than mine. I've wanted to learn and have them motivate me like role models."

Whether in parenting or career, Eni tries to take those examples and apply them to her busy life.

In a community, we also have the opportunity to pour into the lives of others. There are times when we may feel like we are receiving more than we are giving, and there are times when we are simply available to others. We have all known people whom we would classify as either givers or takers; however, a healthy community includes both. Being mindful of the rhythms of giving and taking will help us be intentional in both and afford us the ability to do both.

INTEGRATING IN COMMUNITY

Sometimes life is stressful at home when things seem to be going well at work, and sometimes the reverse is true. A community of peers is a place where we see ourselves more clearly. Being self-aware is a sign of emotional maturity, and being with others who share our struggles and joys in life helps us to see where we need to pay closer attention.

Eni talks about her group. "By sharing with others the stories of our lives, we see that there are other people like us out there who balance their lives. They are moms with kids but are very good in their professional life. They also have the spirit of 'at the end of the day, you just yield to God, and he knows better.'"

SHARED VALUES

One of the key communities in Eni's life is with her team, her employees. The hotel emphasizes integrity as a key value, and this was put to the test in a recent event.

A guest had forgotten her AirPods at the hotel. They couldn't find them at the moment when the guest had to leave, so they emailed her that they would ship them these tiny electronic headphones to her when they found them.

The housekeeping staff found the AirPods, but meanwhile the guest, obviously feeling she wasn't going to see her property again, left the hotel and gave them a 2 rating on a social media site. The front desk workers didn't want to send the AirPods back as the guest had given such a poor review after the staff had put so much effort into finding them. Eni reminded them of their value of integrity, and they sent the package. When the guest got the package, she changed the review to an 8.

Eni recalls, "You could see the smiles on their faces at the front desk, that at least what goes around comes around and that we should do our best regardless of the circumstances. It was a good lesson for me, but also for the others."

Eni has developed this community among her employees. This is a family business, and Eni treats the employees like family members. Shared values means more than just stating the values, and community gives them the opportunity to model these values as well.

INTEGRATING THE SPIRITUAL

Eni did not grow up as a church member. But she discovered, and began applying, the spiritual dimension of her life that she learned from her LeaderImpact peers. Integrating her life into a cohesive whole has impacted her relationships and her business.

We gain perspective on life as we learn and apply biblical principles. Integrity, for example, is a biblical value. It also is good business, but as humans, we sometimes need to be reminded of what is really important. It is good business to treat others the way we would like to be treated, even when it takes an extra effort. Knowing and applying these biblical values is important to us as individuals and as a community, even when we don't see the results.

COMMUNITY CREATES CULTURE

Every business has a culture, for good or bad. Encouraging each other to live by your stated values consistently creates a culture that reflects those values. In a corporate culture like a hotel, knowing the values is the first step. Living by those values happens as the community, or group of employees, acts intentionally and consistently over time. Culture, by definition, is not an individual thing but rather a group thing. We need community in order to embed the desired culture in our businesses.

COMMUNITY REQUIRES FORGIVENESS

People make mistakes. Being part of a community means we hold ourselves, and each other, accountable, and this will inevitably mean we need to forgive others. Eni learned this important lesson at her hotel and shares her wisdom.

"Just treat the employees as human beings first of all. We know they have flaws, issues, and problems. We treat them with dignity, no matter what they do. We've even had employees that stole from our business. This is our strength as a company. We have a very low turnover because we give second chances and treat them with dignity. We try to understand our employees, because at the end of the day, we make profit through them. We should give back to them and the least we can do is treat them well."

Of course, there are limits. Some employees will refuse to embrace the culture. Some will continue to behave improperly. Knowing when it is in the best interests of the business and the other employees to terminate someone is also a part of good leadership. Treating individuals with dignity does not mean suffering through their improper behavior over time. Community and treating others with dignity can even mean laying off someone when you see that they cannot grow or adapt to the culture of your business.

IT'S LONELY AT THE TOP

As mentioned above, Eni is part of a LeaderImpact group, along with other leaders in Tirana. In addition to learning from Eni about leading in community at her work, being a part of a group outside her work connects her to other leaders and is a core part of her growing personally, professionally, and spiritually to have an impact in her work community.

When we ask people what they like the most about being part of a LeaderImpact Group, the most common answer is, "Not being alone." It parallels that one of the biggest challenges leaders face is loneliness. The statement "It's lonely at the top" is, sadly, too true. However, we find that as part of a regular LeaderImpact group, there is strength in being part of a community or peers who may share similar struggles. The group can become a safe place to process life and support each other in our various arenas of leadership. Here are some quotes from my first LeaderImpact group:

> Sometimes it's lonely at the top; that comes with the territory. However, I had to change my stance on this. Through regular interactions with other leaders, and some of the excellent resources, I have realized that I can have the power to change this. (Sam, VP Marketing, Analytics start-up)

> I've really enjoyed learning some fantastic leadership principles and being able to share and bounce ideas off of the other group members who have different experiences and insights. (Russ, General Manager, Fintech Company)

> It's a positive community that inspires you to challenge yourself to become a better leader. (Andrew, Director, Insurance Brokerage)

> The most valuable aspect of our LeaderImpact group is having a trusted, confidential group of leaders outside of my regular workplace, to learn, grow, and discuss life challenges with. (Chris, Senior HR Director)

AN UNCOMMON OPPORTUNITY

There are many opportunities that come our way, and some may seem more compelling than others, but perhaps the ones we ought to take up are the ones that really seem uncommon, unique, rare.

Sales, deals, and experiences are opportunities that seem to come along pretty regularly. What is truly uncommon? As a leader, what is something that is truly rare?

I want to suggest to you that as a leader, being part of a community or group of other leaders to process life together is a truly uncommon opportunity! It is common to toil alone as a leader. The *uncommon opportunity* is to team up with others.

As part of my LeaderImpact group, we essentially do a few things each week. We read a chapter of a great leadership book and discuss it together. And there are also periodic opportunities to host a guest speaker, attend a conference or webinar, or socialize together. There is even the chance to exchange with other leaders around the world.

Are these uncommon things? In and of themselves, these things may not be uncommon. Anyone can read a good book. As Solomon the Wise once said, "Of making many books there is no end, and much study wearies the body."[33] We can also discuss things all day long, and there are a plethora of conferences or webinars we could attend!

Yet we keep coming back to be together week after week. Why? I think it's the combination of doing these things *together* in affinity with others whom we are growing in relationship with.

It is not uncommon to do any of the things listed above. What is uncommon is to be able to do some of these things *with* others—peers, people with similar challenges—and be able to interact and share them together on a regular basis. Through LeaderImpact groups, I have been able to meet some of the most incredible people and hear their stories and perspectives.

Many leaders find themselves in a lonely place. They can't easily process their challenges with people around them, such as employees, team members, and often friends and family who may not understand their context. But other leaders often do get it. They can relate, empathize, and even help with solutions and encouragement.

We live in such a fast-paced world that it can be hard to keep up with life's regular commitments, and so one of the truly uncommon opportunities in life may, in fact, be the opportunity to take a step back and invest in yourself as a leader. Allow yourself the luxury of time to grow and be refreshed by others.

So yes, this is a pitch for inviting you to consider joining a LeaderImpact group if you are a leader and are not already part of a group. You can find out more at LeaderImpact.com. Whether you are like Eni in Tirana, Albania, or like me in Auckland, New Zealand, you can team up with others and join a LeaderImpact group.

However, more than this, I want to encourage you to find your space where you can seek out the wisdom of others, learn from them, and also offer them something. Invest and give to others as you receive yourself. Find a community that fits your affinities and people that are part of your "tribe" and get involved. Sign up. Participate. Learn. Grow. Flourish.

Often we just hunker down and try to manage life on our own, in our own heads—this is common. Or we try to "escape" from our situations hoping the next trip, holiday, or buzz will take our mind off things for a while.

What is uncommon is intentionally teaming up with a few other quality people who can mutually invest in each other.

As Solomon the Wise also said:

> Again I saw something meaningless under the sun:
>
> There was a man all alone; he had neither son nor brother.
>
> There was no end to his toil, yet his eyes were not content with his wealth.
>
> "For whom am I toiling," he asked, "and why am I depriving myself of enjoyment?"
>
> This too is meaningless—a miserable business!
>
> Two are better than one, because they have a good return for their labor:
>
> If either of them falls down, one can help the other up.
>
> But pity anyone who falls and has no one to help them up.
>
> Also, if two lie down together, they will keep warm.
>
> But how can one keep warm alone?

Though one may be overpowered, two can defend themselves.

A cord of three strands is not quickly broken.³⁴

***

Questions for Discussion:

1. In what ways do you lead in community with others?
2. Which of the principles Eni shared are most relevant for you now?
3. To whom do you go to when you need encouragement or counsel?
4. Are you part of a regular group sharing with other leaders? If not, what's stopping you? Go on, sign up for a group today at LeaderImpact.com!

10
POSITIVE IMPACT

If you remain in me and I in you, you will bear much fruit.

—Jesus[35]

Congratulations on making it to the final chapter!

Through our time together in this book, we have focused on how as leaders we can live a fruitful and integrated life—bringing together the personal, professional, and spiritual sides of our lives and considering how they apply to a number of key areas and issues we may face as leaders.

We have also met a number of great leaders and learned from their example of living an integrated life. In each instance, the questions remain: What is the purpose of this story as it relates to my life? What is next?

I believe the core purpose of our growth as leaders is not so we can rest on our accomplishments, but rather, it is so we can have a positive impact on the world around us.

It sounds good, right? But what does it actually mean?

This final chapter is designed to help us think about a framework for how we can apply some of what we have learned to our own integrated life as leaders.

POSITIVE

My assumption is that as leaders, we desire to have a *positive* impact on the world around us. No good leader wants to deliberately have a negative impact on their families, communities, companies, organizations, or cities. However, it is important to think about this intentionally as all leaders create ripples around them, and our impact is never neutral. Being unintentional may mean we could be leaving a negative wake in some areas, so it's important to be self-aware and focused on creating positive impact.

IMPACT

What does *impact* mean in practice? One dictionary says that impact is "to have a strong effect on someone or something."

Positive impact, then, is about having a sustained and positive effect or influence on people, groups of people, an organization, or culture.

THE INTEGRATED LIFE

LeaderImpact's mission statement is to "help leaders grow personally, professionally, and spiritually for increasing impact. We desire positive, intentional, integrated, and progressive impact—that is, it begins within the leader, but it doesn't stop there. That impact is purposefully moving from the leader outward to those closest to them, then to their sphere of influence, and finally to the broader society.

Just as we can think of our growth as a leader in personal, professional, and spiritual terms, we can also look at our impact in similar terms. Perhaps you can use this framework to consider your impact and legacy.

- *Personally.* In leaders having stronger families as they become better spouses and parents. In deeper, more significant relationships that benefit not only the leader but the other person. In leaders becoming more "others-centered," taking steps to serve others at home, in their workplace, and in their communities. In leaders who are uncommonly generous with their time, gifts, and finances.

- *Professionally.* In the way leaders run their businesses, leading with excellence and integrity but also compassion and unselfishness. In the way they treat their employees, such that it is noticeable inside and out. In leaders leveraging their vocation, influence, and resources to serve their community. In signs of positive change within their domain and within their cities/countries.

- *Spiritually.* In more leaders pursuing a spiritual journey, coming into an understanding of God's purpose for our lives, to knowing Jesus, and to being filled and empowered by his Spirit. In leaders who demonstrate a growing understanding and practice of the Spirit-filled life within their daily lives. In leaders who are developing some healthy spiritual practices. In leaders who are regularly taking faith risks of some kind.

As I was writing this section, I met a new friend who is having a positive impact all around him. He is part of the local chamber of commerce in his city, runs an orphanage, pastors a church, and is raising his family—talk about having a personal, professional, and spiritual impact! Not all of us are called to have such radical commitments at the same time, but we can each consider how we can have a positive impact.

Let's explore each of these aspects a little more . . .

PERSONAL IMPACT

Impact can first of all be thought of personally in terms of the people that we impact—whether they be family, friends, close connections, colleagues, employers, employees, or acquaintances.

A number of the leaders in this book have talked about personal impact—in terms of our home relationships, community opportunities, coping with stress, or leading in our financial stewardship.

What is the impact you are creating personally? In your key relationships?

In his book *Becoming a Leader of Impact*, Braden Douglas describes impact in terms of leadership as "influence that inspires others towards perpetual positive behavior."

In his book, Braden also recommends a reflection exercise where we create a list of the core relationships that we have and consider our impact in them. This is a great but challenging exercise! You can list your immediate family, extended family, and professional and social connections, identify your most key relationships, and ask for each one:

- What is their personal purpose or goal?
- What is one thing I can do to help them with that?

This kind of intentionality can result in a simple yet profound positive impact in people's lives.

PROFESSIONAL IMPACT

A second aspect is having an impact professionally.

A number of our chapters have focused in this arena—considering our impact in work, business, handling risks or success, or handling hard conversations in our organizations.

We spend much of our time working, and while we may be doing a good job and generating an income, we can sometimes limit the extent of our impact professionally.

I have noticed that people often think about their impact at work, or through their profession, in terms of being a good worker, being a leader of high integrity, and generally a nice person who cares about the well-being of others and their organization.

This is certainly the right place to start, but it is not sufficient to leave it there. I believe we were created for more! As my friend Steven Garber writes in his book *Visions of Vocation*:

> Vocation is integral, not incidental to the Missio Dei.[36]

Or in my words, our vocation—our calling, our life's work—is integral to what God has placed us on this earth for and central to God's mission in the world. Imagine that! Our vocation and daily work is central to what God is doing in the world!

This does not just include so-called "spiritual" or "religious" work, or even "good works" like social justice or helping people—though these must be included for sure. There are many needs and causes in the world, and we need leaders to create a positive impact in these arenas. However, positive impact also includes all the good work that is necessary for the working and well-being of a civil society and a good and functioning world.

God is integrally invested in our daily work—be it leading, accounting, marketing, financing, banking, coding, teaching, engineering, governing, farming, gardening, and more. In fact, gardening is probably the first work God gave humans in the Bible in Genesis. God's first commissioning of us as humans from the beginning was to work, to rule over the world, and take care of it.[37]

Whether you are a "butcher, baker, or candlestick maker," all are avenues and opportunities for creating positive impact. And not just by being a nice and honest butcher, baker, or candlestick maker, but also by creating great cuts of meat, making great bread, and crafting excellent candles. Before Jesus was a great teacher and miracle worker, he was a carpenter—and I suspect he made great tables. And God was pleased with it.

Andy Crouch, in his book *Culture Making*, says a key part of our work is to be creators of culture, not just "consumers, critics, or condemners" of it.[38]

Through our professional lives, our day-to-day work, we can be part of leading and creating lasting and sustained positive impact on the world. By working in our professions to the best of our ability, we can influence them by bringing needed positive change.

- To be a good lawyer is not just to be an honest and efficient one—you can be a bearer of justice.

- To be a good teacher is not just to be an honest and efficient one—you can be an agent of learning.

- To be a good farmer is not just to be an honest and efficient one—you can feed the world.

- To be a good builder is not just to be an honest and efficient one—you can be a provider of great homes.

- And to be a champion of important causes where positive change is greatly needed is also to reflect the "*Missio Dei.*"

Together, this is how we impact the world for good professionally. Our occupation is not just a paycheck. It is a place for creating positive impact. How can you see your profession as a place for sustained and positive influence?

SPIRITUAL IMPACT

Now, let's consider the spiritual.

We started this book talking about the "wind in our sails," the Spirit-filled, integrated life. I believe people are eternal. We are spiritual beings. And this influences every other aspect of our lives and leadership.

To have a positive spiritual impact is perhaps a combination of the personal and professional, with the added dimensions of eternity and the spiritual reality. Both our personal and professional impacts can be motivated by our spiritual lives. For example, we may be motivated to care for those around us or make our organization a great place to work because of God's command to love others.

My grandfather probably had the greatest spiritual impact on me. He recalls being a young man of nineteen, standing at his own father's grave, and concluding, "This cannot be the end!"

As he explored the nature of life and death, he became a follower of Jesus and encouraged many others as well. As a builder, farmer, and father of eleven, he also began a church in our small town. He had a wide impact for sure, but to me, he was the man who challenged me to consider the spiritual side of life.

I remember going to him when I was about nineteen and sharing my questions about faith, and he said, "Roger, if you need to find the answers to everything, you will probably not end up doing anything."

I didn't want to be someone who didn't do anything, paralyzed by indecision. So I learned to put my trust in the "answers I couldn't question," rather than remain caught in the "questions I couldn't answer." I knew many things to be true, so I put my faith in God and decided to trust him as I explored more of the answers, and I have never looked back.

Recognizing that our existence on this earth is not all there is to life also puts our life span in greater perspective. Knowing we are to spend eternity either in God's presence or separated from him causes us to evaluate our life and leadership from a spiritual and eternal perspective.

I believe the greatest discovery we can make is to know God through his Son, Jesus. To help others get to know God also—and discover their potential as a spiritual being—is the greatest thing we can engage in with others. This is an eternally positive impact!

Where are you in your spiritual journey? How does it affect your impact personally, professionally, and as a leader? How can you influence others toward spiritual growth?

MAXIMUM IMPACT

Finally, it can be helpful to mentally consider the personal, professional, and spiritual separately as we have done, but it is only when we are seeking to grow and lead in an integrated way that we can have our best impact. In reality, we cannot separate them. Our personal lives overflow into our work, and our spiritual perspectives influence all of our life and leadership.

The sweet spot for our impact is at the intersection of our personal, professional, and spiritual leadership.

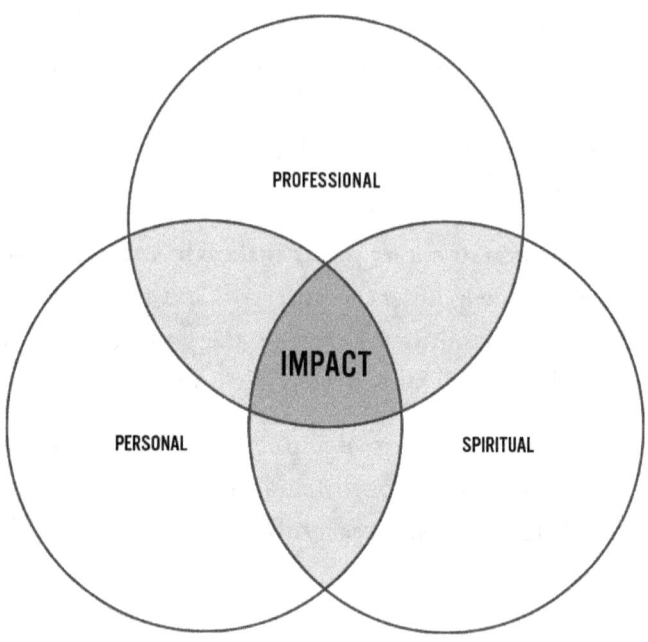

As you consider your life and leadership, is there a point of intersection that you can see where these things come together? What is your "sweet spot"?

One of the things I love to do is being in mentoring relationships with people. I find that in these types of relationships and conversations, I can engage my professional skills in leadership and life direction, challenge our faith and spiritual growth, and share personal stories of life experiences. I think that's a sweet spot for me, a positive impact in others' lives and my own.

How about you? What would you like to do next?

POSITIVE IMPACT STARTS HERE!

In LeaderImpact, we also like to use the phrase "Positive impact starts here!"

There are a couple of ways I see this working out:

First, positive impact starts in our own lives as leaders. What goes on "inside" eventually works its way "outside." The most important aspects of life for a leader is to be integrated inside for positive impact to start in our own lives. To be transformed from the inside out. To be growing personally, professionally, and also spiritually. As in chapter 1, where we talked about the importance of the spiritual side of life and letting the Spirit of God "fill us," empower us, and guide us, like the wind does to a sail. This is the real secret to a life of maximum impact.

Second, positive impact starts in our own spheres of influence. Many leaders are not living out their maximum impact. They are burdened down by the worries of life, pressures of being the perfect family person, leading at work, and for many, seeking to serve their community, perhaps through a church or other group. Yet I believe that if as leaders we can truly grasp the power of a fully integrated life, positive impact is going to bring positive change to every corner, sector, and home on the planet. The world is yet to see the impact of a generation of leaders joining together to see positive impact in the world.

I believe the greatest change for good in the world could be sparked by marketplace leaders from around the world joining to grow together, supporting each other, and making a difference in the world!

As we conclude, this is my challenge to you:

Before you close this book, would you take some extra time now to reflect on your impact?

Positive impact starts with us.

* * *

Questions for Discussion

1. What are some ideas that come to mind for how you can have an increasing positive impact?
   - Personally?
   - Professionally?
   - Spiritually?
2. What will you do first?

ABOUT LEADERIMPACT

LeaderImpact has been inspiring and developing leaders for decades. Their purpose as a global organization is to help leaders develop professionally, personally, and spiritually in order to have an impact.

Leaders meet together in groups on a regular basis to work through LeaderImpact curriculum, which is typically based on popular business and leadership books by authors such as Jim Collins, Patrick Lencioni, Simon Sinek, and others. Groups are facilitated by volunteer leaders who have great real-world experience and who buy into the core values of the organization.

What sets LeaderImpact apart from the myriad of networking or peer groups is their focus on holistic development for the leader (professional, personal, and spiritual) and their focus on outreach. It's not enough for leaders to stay insulated in these groups. It's about growth and inviting other leaders to experience the same life change.

Each participating city runs LeaderImpact forums, which are events designed to bring together the influential leaders within an area. These forums typically feature a great speaker in an upscale venue to ensure a great experience.

Each year there are multiple trips to countries that are starting LeaderImpact. Experienced leaders have the opportunity to present great content from their area of expertise but also share where impact comes from. I've had the privilege of speaking and working with leaders in numerous countries around the world. I'd love for you to experience the same thing.

Even though the organization is active in over twenty-five countries, it's still in its infancy stage. We need great leaders, like you, to get on board and leverage your time, influence, and resources to propel it forward.

This is what being part of a movement is about. You can help us.

Sometimes you just need a little push.

You can find out more, start a group, or get involved at LeaderImpact.com.

ACKNOWLEDGMENTS

This book has been a team effort. I am indebted to the work of the team at LeaderImpact and the leaders who offered to share their stories with us. Thank you! Any errors are mine. The credit is yours.

My heartfelt thanks go to Meredith Stuart and Ed Maggard, who did most of the research, interviewing, and drafting of each leader's personal story in many of the chapters. Meredith also served as the project manager for this book, investing her leadership talent in organizing, arranging, editing, publishing, and marketing. Thank you both!

I also want to thank my wife, Nicki, who has not only been a great source of encouragement to me and providing feedback, but she also undertook the marketing and promotion of the book. Thank you, my love!

Thank you also to Matthew Coyle and Judy Hildebrandt, who provided editorial assistance and feedback—thank you for making this book so much better.

Thank you to the team at Gatekeeper Press—Rob, Jennifer, and Faith—for your editorial support and publishing expertise. You have helped us get across the finish line, and it has been a pleasure to work together.

Finally, thank you to all the team at LeaderImpact for your dedicated service to leaders around the world—"positive impact starts here"!

ABOUT THE AUTHOR

Roger is passionate about helping leaders grow personally, professionally, and spiritually. He enjoys speaking to leaders about the significant role they can play through their work in the world and how they can be a part of a global movement of leaders making a positive impact in their spheres of influence.

LeaderImpact is a global nonprofit organization active in over seventy countries, and Roger has served as the executive director from 2019 to 2023. He has led several large multinational teams that host events and provides resources focused on leadership development.

Roger studied economics, politics, and geography at the University of Auckland and worked in trade economic analysis for the New Zealand government before joining the nonprofit sector.

Roger is happily married to his wife, Nicki. They live in the northern part of Auckland, New Zealand. They have two adult sons, Alex and William. Roger enjoys great food and coffee, especially in new cities around the world.

rogerosbaldiston.com

ENDNOTES

1. Braden Douglas, *Becoming a Leader of Impact: How Your Influence Can Change the World* (LeaderImpact Publishing, 2020).

2. Dictionary.com, accessed February 1, 2023, https://www.dictionary.com/.

3. Jackson H. Brown, *Life's Little Instruction Book* (Nashville: Rutledge Hill Press, 1991).

4. Crosby, Stills, Nash & Young, *CSN 2012* (CSN Records, 2012).

5. LeaderImpact resources can be found at LeaderImpact.com.

6. Acts 27, New International Version, Abridged.

7. 2 Peter 1:21, New International Version.

8. Rick Warner, "Tall Man Tyrell Biggs Thinks His Height Will Add New Dimension to Fight," *The Orangeburg Times and Democrat* (August 19, 1987).

9. David Whyte, *Midlife and the Great Unknown: Finding Courage and Clarity Through Poetry.* (Boulder: Sounds True, 2003).

10. Bill Bright, *Transferable Concepts* (Arrowhead Springs: Campus Crusade for Christ Interntional, 1981).

11. John 8:32, New International Version.

12. "Alan Kay Quotes," BrainyQuote.com, BrainyMedia Inc. 2023, accessed February 13, 2023, https://www.brainyquote.com/quotes/alan_kay_100831.

13. Jack Welch and Suzy Welch, *Winning: The Answers: Confronting 74 of the Toughest Questions in Business Today* (New York: Collins, 2007).
14. https://rogerosbaldiston.com/articles/2020/10/13/leading-an-elephant.
15. Chip Heath and Dan Heath, *Switch: How to Change Things When Change Is Hard* (New York: Random House US, 2010).
16. Brené Brown, *Dare to Lead. Brave Work. Tough Conversations. Whole Hearts* (New York: Random House, 2018).
17. Joni Eareckson Tada, "Vain Imaginations: Joni and Friends," *Joni and Friends*, August 1, 2022, https://www.joniandfriends.org/vain-imaginations/.
18. Edson Arantes do Nascimento, Twitter, @Pele (July 22, 2014), twitter.com/Pele.
19. LeaderImpact resources can be found at LeaderImpact.com.
20. *ABBA: Gold (Greatest Hits)* (Polar, 1992).
21. Matthew 6:21, New International Version.
22. www.RiseAboveFinance.com.
23. Mark Gumm, "Financial Peace and the Miracle of Adoption," YouTube, December 7, 2009, https://www.youtube.com/watch?v=-mGEn_EiljI.
24. 2 Corinthians 9:6, New International Version.
25. J. Johnson, "10 Warren Buffett Quotes Every Business Owner Needs to Hear," US Chamber of Commerce, January 27, 2020, retrieved February 13, 2023, https://www.uschamber.com/co/

start/strategy/warren-buffett-quotes-for-businesses.

26. Garth Jestley. *More Than Your Business Card: A Wake-Up Call for Leaders Desiring to Follow Jesus in the Marketplace* (Austin: The Fedd Agency Inc., 2021).

27. Stephen R. Covey, Twitter, @StephenRCovey (October 12, 2017), www.twitter.com/stephenrcovey.

28. Packard Foundation, Twitter, @PackardFDN (September 7, 2022), twitter.com/packardfdn.

29. Andrew Wommack. "Andrew Wommack Devotional 3rd November 2022—Chosen before Creation," TheDevotionals.com.ng, November 3, 2022, https://www.thedevotionals.com.ng/andrew-wommack-devotional-tuesday-3rd-november-2020-chosen-before-creation/.

30. John C. Maxwell, *Today Matters: 12 Daily Practices to Guarantee Tomorrow's Success* (New York: Time Warner Book Group, 2004).

31. Keith and Esther Dindi, *Thriving Couples: Keeping Marriage Fun and Fulfilling* (Nairobi, Kenya: Zion Pearl Publishers, 2021).

32. Jack Johnson, "Better Together," *In Between Dreams* (Brushfire Records, 2005).

33. Ecclesiastes 12:12, New International Version.

34. Ecclesiastes 4:7–12, New International Version.

35. John 15:5, New International Version.

36. Steven Garber, *Visions of Vocation: Common Grace for the*

Common Good (Downers Grove: IVP Books, an imprint of InterVarsity Press, 2014).

37. Genesis 1–2, The Bible, Old Testament.

38. Andy Crouch, *Culture Making: Recovering Our Creative Calling* (Westmont: InterVarsity Press, 2013).

WOULD YOU LIKE TO
Know God Personally?

Millions of people around the world have discovered a relationship with God through the truths explored in this booklet. The following four principles describe how anyone can know God personally and experience the abundant life He promised.

GOD'S LOVE

1. God <u>loves</u> you and created you to know Him personally. He offers a wonderful <u>plan</u> for your life.

GOD'S LOVE
"For God so loved the world that He gave His one and only Son, that whoever believes in Him shall not perish but have eternal life." JOHN 3:16

GOD'S PLAN
"Now this is eternal life: that they know You, the only true God, and Jesus Christ, whom You have sent." JOHN 17:3

→ *What prevents us from knowing God personally?*

GOD'S LOVE

5

OUR CONDITION

2. *People are <u>sinful</u> and <u>separated</u> from God, so we cannot know Him personally or experience His love and plan.*

OUR CONDITION

PEOPLE ARE SINFUL
"...all have sinned and fall short of the glory of God."
ROMANS 3:23

People were created to have fellowship with God; but, because of our stubborn self-will, we chose to go our own independent way and fellowship with God was broken. This self-will, characterized by an attitude of active rebellion or passive indifference, is evidence of what the Bible calls sin.

PEOPLE ARE SEPARATED
"For the wages of sin is death..." ROMANS 6:23
[spiritual separation from God]

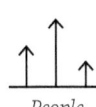

This diagram illustrates that God is holy and people are sinful. A great chasm separates the two. The arrows illustrate that we are continually trying to reach God and establish a personal relationship with Him through our own efforts, such as a good life, philosophy or religion, but we inevitably fail.

→ *The third principle explains the only way to bridge this gap...*

3. *Jesus Christ is God's only <u>provision</u> for our sin. Through Him <u>alone</u> we can know God personally and experience His love and plan.*

8

GOD'S RESPONSE

HE DIED IN OUR PLACE
"But God demonstrates His own love for us in this: While we were still sinners, Christ died for us." ROMANS 5:8

HE ROSE FROM THE DEAD
"...Christ died for our sins...He was buried...He was raised on the third day according to the Scriptures...He appeared to Cephas, and then to the Twelve. After that, He appeared to more than five hundred..."
1 CORINTHIANS 15:3-6

HE IS THE ONLY WAY TO GOD
"Jesus answered, 'I am the way and the truth and the life. No one comes to the Father except through Me." JOHN 14:6

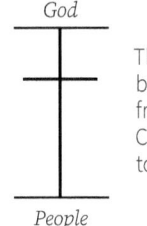

This diagram illustrates that God has bridged the chasm that separates us from Him by sending His Son, Jesus Christ, to die on the cross in our place to pay the penalty for our sins.

→ *It is not enough just to know these truths...*

OUR RESPONSE

4. We must individually <u>receive</u> Jesus Christ as Savior and Lord; then we can <u>know</u> God personally and experience His love and plan.

WE MUST RECEIVE CHRIST
"Yet to all who did receive Him, to those who believed in His name, He gave the right to become children of God." JOHN 1:12

WE RECEIVE CHRIST THROUGH FAITH
"For it is by grace you have been saved, through faith—and this is not from yourselves, it is the gift of God—not by works, so that no one can boast." EPHESIANS 2:8-9

WHEN WE RECEIVE CHRIST, WE EXPERIENCE A NEW BIRTH
READ JOHN 3:1-8

OUR RESPONSE

→ *The following explains how you can receive Christ...*

OUR RESPONSE

WE RECEIVE CHRIST BY PERSONAL INVITATION
[Christ speaking] "Here I am! I stand at the door and knock. If anyone hears My voice and opens the door, I will come in and eat with that person, and they with Me." REVELATION 3:20

Receiving Christ involves turning to God from self (repentance) and trusting Christ to come into our lives to forgive us of our sins and to make us who He wants us to be. Just to agree intellectually that Jesus Christ is the Son of God and that He died on the cross for our sins is not enough. Nor is it enough to have an emotional experience. We receive Jesus Christ by faith, as an act of our will.

OUR RESPONSE

THESE TWO CIRCLES REPRESENT TWO KINDS OF LIVES

A LIFE WITHOUT JESUS CHRIST
Self is central and on the throne and Jesus Christ is on the outside.

A LIFE ENTRUSTED TO CHRIST
Christ is central and on the throne, and self yields to Christ.

→ *Which circle best represents your life?*
→ *Which circle would you like to have represent your life?*

HOW YOU CAN RECEIVE CHRIST

YOU CAN RECEIVE CHRIST RIGHT NOW BY FAITH THROUGH PRAYER (PRAYER IS TALKING WITH GOD) God knows your heart and is not as concerned with your words as He is with the attitude of your heart. The following is a suggested prayer:

> *Lord Jesus, I need You. Thank You for dying on the cross for my sins. I open the door of my life and receive You as my Savior and Lord. Thank You for forgiving my sins and giving me eternal life. Take control of the throne of my life. Make me the kind of person You want me to be.*

14

HOW YOU CAN RECEIVE CHRIST

→ *Does this prayer express the desire of your heart?*

If it does, pray this prayer right now, and Christ will come into your life, as He promised.

→ *Did you recieve Christ into your life?*

According to His promise as recorded in Revelation 3:20, where is Christ right now in relation to you?

Christ said that He would come into your life and be your Savior and friend so you can know Him personally. Would He mislead you? On what authority do you know that God has answered your prayer? (The trustworthiness of God Himself and His Word.)

→ *To enjoy your new relationship with God...*

THE BIBLE PROMISES ETERNAL LIFE TO ALL WHO RECEIVE CHRIST

"And this is the testimony: God has given us eternal life, and this life is in His Son. Whoever has the Son has life; whoever does not have the Son of God does not have life. I write these things to you who believe in the name of the Son of God so that you may know that you have eternal life." 1 JOHN 5:11-13

Thank God often that Christ is in your life and that He will never leave you (HEBREWS 13:5).

You can know on the basis of His promise that Christ lives in you and that you have eternal life from the very moment you invite Him in.

AN IMPORTANT REMINDER

The promise of God's Word, the Bible—not our feelings—is our authority. The Christian lives by faith (trust) in the character of God Himself and His Word. This train diagram illustrates the relationship between fact (God and His Word), faith (our trust in God and His Word), and feeling (the result of our faith and obedience) (JOHN 14:21).

ENJOYING YOUR NEW RELATIONSHIP WITH GOD

The train will run with or without the caboose. However, it would be useless to attempt to pull the train by the caboose. In the same way, we as Christians do not depend on feelings or emotions, but we place our faith (trust) in the character of God and the promises of His Word.

NOW THAT YOU HAVE ENTERED INTO A PERSONAL RELATIONSHIP WITH CHRIST

The moment you received Christ by faith, as an act of your will, many things happened, including the following:

- Christ came into your life. (REVELATION 3:20; COLOSSIANS 1:27)
- Your sins were forgiven. (COLOSSIANS 1:14)
- You became a child of God. (JOHN 1:12)
- You received eternal life. (JOHN 5:24)
- You began the great adventure for which God created you. (JOHN 10:10; 2 CORINTHIANS 5:17; 1 THESSALONIANS 5:18)

ENJOYING YOUR NEW RELATIONSHIP WITH GOD

Can you think of anything more wonderful that could happen to you than entering into a personal relationship with Jesus Christ? Would you like to thank God in prayer right now for what He has done for you? By thanking God, you demonstrate your faith.

SUGGESTIONS FOR CHRISTIAN GROWTH
Spiritual growth results from trusting Jesus Christ. "…The righteous will live by faith" (GALATIANS 3:11). A life of faith will enable you to trust God increasingly with every detail of your life, and to practice the following:

G   Go to God in prayer daily. (JOHN 15:7)

R   Read God's Word daily. Begin with the Gospel of John. (ACTS 17:11)

O   Obey God moment by moment. (JOHN 14:21)

W   Witness for Christ by your life and words. (MATTHEW 4:19 AND JOHN 15:8)

T   Trust God for every detail of your life. (1 PETER 5:7)

H   Holy Spirit—allow Him to control and empower your daily life and witness. (GALATIANS 5:16,17; ACTS 1:8)

ENJOYING YOUR NEW RELATIONSHIP WITH GOD

REMEMBER...
Your walk with Christ depends on what you allow Him to do in and through you, empowered by the Holy Spirit, not what you do for Him through self effort.

FELLOWSHIP IN A GOOD CHURCH
Several logs burn brightly together, but put one aside on the cold hearth and the fire goes out. So it is with your relationship with other Christians. If you do not belong to a church, do not wait to be invited. Take the initiative; call the pastor of a nearby church where Christ is honored and His Word is preached. Start this week, and make plans to attend regularly.

HAVE YOU MADE THE WONDERFUL DISCOVERY *of* THE SPIRIT-FILLED LIFE?

EVERY DAY CAN BE an exciting adventure for the Christian who knows the reality of being filled with the Holy Spirit and who lives constantly, moment by moment, under His gracious direction.

The Bible tells us that there are three kinds of people:

1. NATURAL PERSON
(One who has not received Christ)

Self-Directed Life
S – Self is on the throne
†– Christ is outside the life
● – Interests are directed by self, often resulting in discord and frustration

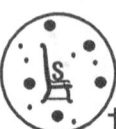

"A natural man does not accept the things of the Spirit of God; for they are foolishness to him, and he cannot understand them, because they are spiritually appraised."
(1 CORINTHIANS 2:14)

2. SPIRITUAL PERSON
(One who is directed and empowered by the Holy Spirit)

Christ-Directed Life
†– Christ is in the life and on the throne
S – Self is yielding to Christ
● – Interests are directed by Christ, resulting in harmony with God's plan

"He who is spiritual appraises all things...We have the mind of Christ." (1 CORINTHIANS 2:15,16)

3. WORLDLY (CARNAL) PERSON

(One who has received Christ, but who lives in defeat because he is trying to live the Christian life in his own strength)

Self-Directed Life
S – Self is on the throne
† – Christ dethroned and not allowed to direct the life
● – Interests are directed by self, often resulting in discord and frustration

"Brothers, I could not address you as spiritual but as worldly—mere infants in Christ. I gave you milk, not solid food, for you were not yet ready for it. Indeed, you are still not ready. You are still worldly. For since there is jealousy and quarreling among you, are you not worldly? Are you not acting like mere men?"
(1 CORINTHIANS 3:1-3, NIV)

The following are four principles for living the Spirit-filled life.

1

> *God has provided for us an abundant and fruitful Christian life.*

JESUS said, "I have come that they may have life, and that they may have it more abundantly." (JOHN 10:10, NKJV)

"I am the vine, you are the branches. He who abides in Me, and I in him, bears much fruit; for without Me you can do nothing." (JOHN 15:5, NKJV)

"The fruit of the Spirit is love, joy, peace, patience, kindness, goodness, faithfulness, gentleness, self-control; against such things there is no law." (GALATIANS 5:22,23)

"You shall receive power when the Holy Spirit has come upon you; and you shall be My witnesses both in Jerusalem, and in all Judea and Samaria, and even to the remotest part of the earth." (ACTS 1:8)

The following are some personal traits of the ***spiritual person*** that result from trusting God:

- Love
- Joy
- Peace
- Patience
- Kindness
- Faithfulness
- Goodness

- Life is Christ-centered
- Empowered by Holy Spirit
- Introduces others to Christ
- Has effective prayer life
- Understands God's Word
- Trusts God
- Obeys God

The degree to which these traits are manifested in the life depends on the extent to which the Christian trusts the Lord with every detail of his life, and on his maturity in Christ. One who is only beginning to understand the ministry of the Holy Spirit should not be discouraged if he is not as fruitful as more mature Christians who have known and experienced this truth for a longer period.

Why is it that most Christians are not experiencing the abundant life?

> *Worldly Christians cannot experience the abundant and fruitful Christian life.*

THE WORLDLY (carnal) person trusts in his own efforts to live the Christian life:

» He is either uninformed about, or has forgotten, God's love, forgiveness, and power.
(ROMANS 5:8-10; HEBREWS 10:1-25; 1 JOHN 1; 2:1-3; 2 PETER 1:9; ACTS 1:8)

» He has an up-and-down spiritual experience.

» He cannot understand himself—he wants to do what is right, but cannot.

" He fails to draw on the power of the Holy Spirit to live the Christian life. (1 CORINTHIANS 3:1-3; ROMANS 7:15-24; 8:7; GALATIANS 5:16-18)

Some or all of the following traits may characterize the *worldly person*—the Christian who does not fully trust God:

- Legalistic attitude
- Impure thoughts
- Jealousy
- Guilt
- Worry
- Discouragement
- Critical spirit
- Frustration
- Aimlessness
- Fear
- Ignorance of his spiritual heritage
- Unbelief
- Disobedience
- Loss of love for God and for others
- Poor prayer life
- No desire for Bible study

(The individual who professes to be a Christian but who continues to practice sin should realize that he may not be a Christian at all, according to 1 John 2:3; 3:6–9; Ephesians 5:5.)

The third truth gives us the only solution to this problem...

3

> *Jesus promised the abundant and fruitful life as the result of being filled (directed and empowered) by the Holy Spirit.*

THE SPIRIT-FILLED LIFE is the Christ-directed life by which Christ lives His life in and through us in the power of the Holy Spirit. (JOHN 15)

» One becomes a Christian through the ministry of the Holy Spirit, according to John 3:1–8. From the moment of spiritual birth, the Christian is indwelt by the Holy Spirit at all times. (JOHN 1:12; COLOSSIANS 2:9,10; JOHN 14:16,17)

Though all Christians are indwelt by the Holy Spirit, not all Christians are filled (directed and empowered) by the Holy Spirit on an ongoing basis.

» The Holy Spirit is the source of the overflowing life. (JOHN 7:37-39)

» The Holy Spirit came to glorify Christ. When one is filled with the Holy Spirit, he is a true disciple of Christ. (JOHN 16:1-15)

» In His last command before His ascension, Christ promised the power of the Holy Spirit to enable us to be witnesses for Him. (ACTS 1:1-9)

How, then, can one be filled with the Holy Spirit?

4

> *We are filled with the Holy Spirit by faith; then we can experience the abundant and fruitful life that Christ promised.*

YOU CAN appropriate the filling of the Holy Spirit *right now* if you:

» Sincerely desire to be directed and empowered by the Holy Spirit. (MATTHEW 5:6; JOHN 7:37-39)

» Confess your sins. By *faith*, thank God that He *has* forgiven all of your sins—past, present, and future—because Christ died for you. (COLOSSIANS 2:13-15; 1 JOHN 1; 2:1-3; HEBREWS 10:1-17)

- Present every area of your life to God.
  (ROMANS 12:1,2)
- By *faith* claim the fullness of the Holy Spirit, according to:

  His command: Be filled with the Spirit.

  "Do not get drunk on wine, which leads to debauchery. Instead, be filled with the Spirit."
  (EPHESIANS 5:18, NIV)

  His promise: He will always answer when we pray according to His will.

  "This is the confidence we have in approaching God: that if we ask anything according to his will, he hears us. And if we know that he hears us—whatever we ask—we know that we have what we asked of him."
  (1 JOHN 5:14,15, NIV)

  Faith can be expressed through prayer...

HOW TO PRAY IN FAITH TO BE FILLED WITH THE HOLY SPIRIT

WE ARE FILLED with the Holy Spirit by _faith_ alone. However, true prayer is one way of expressing our faith. The following is a suggested prayer:

> *Dear Father, I need You. I acknowledge that I have sinned against You by directing my own life. I thank You that You have forgiven my sins through Christ's death on the cross for me. I now invite Christ to again take His place on the throne of my life. Fill me with the Holy Spirit as You* commanded *me to be filled, and as You* promised *in Your Word that You would do if I asked in faith. I pray this in the name of Jesus. As an expression of my faith, I now thank You for directing my life and for filling me with the Holy Spirit.*

Does this prayer express the desire of your heart? If so, bow in prayer and trust God to fill you with the Holy Spirit _right now_.

12

HOW TO KNOW THAT YOU ARE FILLED (DIRECTED AND EMPOWERED) BY THE HOLY SPIRIT

DID YOU ASK God to fill you with the Holy Spirit? Do you know that you are now filled with the Holy Spirit? On what authority? (On the trustworthiness of God Himself and His Word: Hebrews 11:6; John 17:17.)

Do not depend on feelings. The promise of God's Word, not our feelings, is our authority. The Christian lives by faith (trust) in the trustworthiness of God Himself and His Word. This train diagram illustrates the relationship among *fact* (God and His Word), *faith* (our trust in God and His Word), and *feeling* (the result of our faith and obedience). (JOHN 14:21)

The train will run with or without the caboose. However, it would be futile to attempt to pull the train by the caboose. In the same way, we as Christians do not depend on feelings or emotions, but we place our faith (trust) in the trustworthiness of God and the promises of His Word.

HOW TO WALK IN THE SPIRIT

FAITH (trust in God and His promises) is the only way a Christian can live the Spirit-directed life. As you continue to trust Christ moment by moment:

» Your life will demonstrate more and more of the fruit of the Spirit (GALATIANS 5:22,23) and will be more and more conformed to the image of Christ. (ROMANS 12:2; 2 CORINTHIANS 3:18)

» Your prayer life and study of God's Word will become more meaningful.

» You will experience His power in witnessing. (ACTS 1:8)

» You will be prepared for spiritual conflict against the world (1 JOHN 2:15-17); against the flesh. (GALATIANS 5:16,17); and against Satan. (1 PETER 5:7-9; EPHESIANS 6:10-13)

» You will experience His power to resist temptation and sin. (1 CORINTHIANS 10:13; PHILIPPIANS 4:13; EPHESIANS 1:19-23; 2 TIMOTHY 1:7; ROMANS 6:1-16)

SPIRITUAL BREATHING

IF YOU BECOME aware of an area of your life (an attitude or an action) that is displeasing to the Lord, even though you are walking with Him and sincerely desiring to serve Him, simply thank God that He has forgiven your sins—past, present, and future—on the basis of Christ's death on the cross. Claim His love and forgiveness by faith and continue to have fellowship with Him.

If you retake the throne of your life through sin—a definite act of disobedience—breathe spiritually.

Spiritual Breathing (exhaling the impure and inhaling the pure) is an exercise in faith that enables you to experience God's love and forgiveness.

1. **Exhale**: Confess your sin—agree with God concerning your sin and thank Him for His forgiveness of it, according to 1 John 1:9 and Hebrews 10:1–25. Confession involves repentance—a change in attitude and action.

2. **Inhale:** Surrender the control of your life to Christ, and receive the fullness of the-Holy Spirit by faith. Trust that He now directs and empowers you, according to the command of Ephesians 5:18 and the promise of 1 John 5:14,15.

www.ingramcontent.com/pod-product-compliance
Lightning Source LLC
Chambersburg PA
CBHW071242070526
44583CB00017B/2290